THE COMPLETE BIRDHOUSE BOOK

Stokes Nature Guides

by Donald Stokes

A Guide to Nature in Winter
A Guide to Observing Insect Lives
A Guide to Bird Behavior, Volume I

by Donald and Lillian Stokes

A Guide to Bird Behavior, Volume II
A Guide to Bird Behavior, Volume III
A Guide to Enjoying Wildflowers
A Guide to Animal Tracking and Behavior

by Thomas F. Tyning

A Guide to Amphibians and Reptiles

Also by Donald Stokes

The Natural History of Wild Shrubs and Vines

Also by Donald and Lillian Stokes

The Bird Feeder Book
The Hummingbird Book
The Complete Birdhouse Book

THE COMPLETE BIRDHOUSE BOOK

The Easy Guide to Attracting Nesting Birds

Donald and Lillian Stokes

Authors of
Stokes Nature Guides

Illustrations by Donald Stokes
Range Maps by Dianne B. McCorry

Little, Brown and Company

Boston   Toronto   London

First Edition

Library of Congress Cataloging-in-Publication Data

Stokes, Donald W.

    The complete birdhouse book: the easy guide to attracting nesting birds/Donald and Lillian Stokes: illustrations by Donald Stokes: range maps by Dianne B. McCorry. — 1st ed.

        p. cm.

    Includes bibliographical references.

    ISBN 0-316-81714-7

    1. Birds, Attracting of. 2. Birdhouses — Design and construction. 3. Birds — Behavior. I. Stokes, Lillian. II. Title.

QL676.5.S873 1990

598 — dc20   90-30276

                                  CIP

10 9 8 7 6 5 4 3 2 1

RRD-OH

Published simultaneously in Canada by Little, Brown & Company (Canada) Limited

Printed in the United States of America

Photograph Acknowledgments

Animals/Animals: R. H. Armstrong — 17; John Gerlach — 76; Breck P. Kent — 75; Z. Leszczynski — 72; Bates Littlehales — 52; L. L. Rue III — 93; Fred Whitehead — 26.

Bruce Coleman, Inc.: Bob and Clara Calhoun — 51, 63, 78, 87; S. Nielsen — 57; Laura Riley — 84, 86; L. L. Rue III — 89; Joseph Van Wormer — 31; L. West — 53, 71.

Cornell Laboratory of Ornithology: Warren Greene — 61 bottom; Mike Hopiak — 61 top, 70; Steve W. Kress — 58; O. S. Pettingill — 7; Lawrence Wales — 60.

Irene Hinke-Sacilotto: 22 top.

Denny Mallory: 8, 64.

Maslowski Photo: 1, 15, 23, 28, 49, 65, 67, 68, 69, 73, 74, 77, 81, 83, 91.

Myrna D. Pearman: 11, 59.

Photo Researchers: Bob and Elsie Boggs — 62; Anthony Mercieca — 80, 92; William H. Mullins — 27; L. L. Rue III — 79, 85.

Sid Rucker: 6.

Lorne Scott: 66.

Bryan Shantz: 20, 21 top, 21 bottom, 22 bottom.

John Shaw: 19, 88.

Stokes Nature Company: Don and Lillian Stokes/Dianne McCorry — cover, 13, 18, 25, 34, 35, 36, 37, 39 top, 39 bottom, 40, 41, 42, 43, 44, 45.

VIREO: Herbert Clarke — 55; Warren Greene — 56; Betty Randall — 50, 54; Carl Sams II — 10; Barth Schorre — 33.

Mark Wilson: 24.

The authors would like to thank Elsie Eltzroth of Corvallis, Oregon, for supplying them with the breeding information on the western bluebird.

CONTENTS

THE JOYS OF NESTING BIRDS

Many years ago, we decided to try our hand at attracting nesting birds. It was a gray and blustery day in late March, just warm enough so that the ground was partially thawed. There were no signs of birds yet, just us, our boxes, and some posts. We had fun plotting the best locations for each box, but we wondered, as we pounded in the posts, would the birds really come to nest in our meadow?

We put up five birdhouses and then forgot about them until a few days later, when we were driving by the field and saw our first visitor. There, perched on the birdhouse closest to the road and right next to our mailbox, was a beautiful tree swallow.

On our approach, it flew up momentarily. Then, to our excitement, it landed right at the

A young tree swallow nestling in one of our birdhouses calling out for more food from its busy parents.

entrance to the birdhouse, peered in cautiously, rocked in and out several times, and finally went all the way in and looked out at us. We had a prospective tenant!

We were even more excited one morning several days later when we saw two tree swallows sitting on the box, for this meant that we now had a mated pair. We anticipated the joy of watching them raise a family.

Each day brought a new surprise. First we would see the female carrying in strands of dried grasses as she fashioned the nest. The male watched from the top of the box, chasing after any other intruding tree swallows, for others had also arrived at the meadow. At the end of nest building, we saw the female arrive with some beautiful white feathers. Where she had gotten them was a mystery until we later learned that some friends nearby kept chickens.

One day, when we had seen the female fly off to catch insects, we cautiously opened the nest box and discovered five snow-white eggs nestled in the soft feathers. We closed up the box and watched her return and enter to resume incubating. She sat on the eggs for 15 days, in rain, cold, and heat, taking only brief trips away from her precious job to fly around and gather insects for herself and a few times to land on the box, stretch her wings, and preen her feathers.

When both parents began to bring food to the nest, we knew that the babies had hatched. If both parents arrived at once, one would cling patiently to the entrance hole, ducking in when the other one left.

Near the end of the nestling phase, the feeding trips by the parents became more frequent, and we could hear the babies call excitedly when a parent landed on the box. Soon we saw two little

An adult tree swallow in all of its beautiful iridescence.

heads peering out; the babies were now big enough to expectantly survey the world. We could see some jostling occur as first one, then another, vied to look.

Exactly 21 days after the babies had hatched, we were fortunate enough to see the first one leave the birdhouse. It had squeezed so far out of the hole that there was no turning back, so it launched into the air on its first flight. We held our breath, but did not need to worry. By the time they leave the nest, tree swallows are fairly strong flyers, though they are a little clumsy on their first attempts to land.

Soon all of the young had fledged. The family stayed another day or so in the vicinity of the birdhouse, but never went back in it. The young were fed a little by the parents and then became skillful at catching their own insects in midair.

Then one day, when we went out to the field, we saw that they had all left. We missed them, knowing we would have to wait until the next spring to have them again, swooping and soaring over our garden. We wished them a safe migratory journey and a good season in their wintering home, the southern United States coast and Central America. During those months we would clean out their box and make it ready for their return.

Bolstered by our initial success, and addicted to the joy of gaining this intimate view of the family life of the birds, we have, over the years, added greatly to the types and numbers of nesting boxes on our suburban property. We have been fortunate enough to have attracted 12 species of cavity nesters and more than 30 other species of nesting birds.

Given the rapidly increasing destruction of suitable nesting habitats in this day and age, providing nesting boxes not only is a joy for us, but is becoming more and more critical to birds' survival. We need to protect the environment we have and also to provide additional housing and food for the birds.

In this book we will tell you how to make your property a more attractive environment for nesting birds, so that you may have the pleasure of sharing their family life and the knowledge that you are helping to conserve bird populations in this critical time.

We wish you the best of luck!

Don and Lillian Stokes

WHO NESTS WHERE?

Boxing Match

We were recently talking with some friends who told us that they loved goldfinches and wanted to attract them to their yard. They had put up some birdhouses, but no goldfinches were using them. They wondered if they had the wrong type of birdhouse.

Their intentions were wonderful, but they needed to know one important thing about goldfinches — they do not nest in natural cavities or man-made birdhouses; they build open nests in shrubs or trees.

Knowing where birds nest is crucial when you are trying to attract them during the breeding season. Each species has an instinctive pattern of nesting and rarely varies from it. Before you put up boxes to attract certain birds, learn the bird's nesting behavior.

Four Basic Nest Locations

There are four basic locations for nests. Some birds nest in cavities, such as tree holes, birdhouses, or the nooks of buildings. They are called cavity nesters. Common examples are woodpeckers and chickadees.

Many other birds build their nests in the open on branches of shrubs or trees. These nests are generally cup shaped and open to the sky. Such birds are sometimes referred to as open-cup nesters. Common examples are goldfinches, robins, and mockingbirds.

Most of the remaining birds build their nests on the ground, either by constructing an open cup or by scraping just a shallow depression in the earth. Common ground nesters include towhees, killdeers, pheasants, and many sparrows.

A few birds, finally, build their nests underground. A common underground nester is the kingfisher.

The ash-throated flycatcher is one of the birds that is easy to attract with birdhouses. This individual has chosen the rotted-out knothole of a tree as its nest cavity.

Cavity Nesters of North America

This is a complete list of cavity nesters for North America — there are 86 species in all. Not all of these birds always nest in cavities, but all are known to do so at least occasionally.

Some of these birds are easily attracted to birdhouses. Those that are have been marked with asterisks. For a list of common open-cup and ground nesters, see the chapter "Attracting Other Nesting Birds," pages 30–33.

Black-bellied whistling duck
Wood duck*
Common goldeneye*
Barrow's goldeneye*
Bufflehead*
Hooded merganser*
Common merganser*
Turkey vulture
Black vulture
American kestrel*
Merlin
Peregrine falcon
Elegant trogon
Common barn owl*
Barred owl*
Spotted owl
Eastern screech owl*
Western screech owl*
Whiskered screech owl
Flammulated owl
Elf owl
Ferruginous pygmy-owl
Northern pygmy-owl
Northern saw-whet owl*
Northern hawk-owl
Boreal owl
Vaux's swift
Golden-fronted woodpecker*
Red-bellied woodpecker*
Gila woodpecker
Northern flicker*
Red-headed woodpecker*
Acorn woodpecker
White-headed woodpecker
Lewis' woodpecker
Williamson's sapsucker
Red-breasted sapsucker
Yellow-bellied sapsucker

Red-naped sapsucker
Downy woodpecker*
Hairy woodpecker*
Three-toed woodpecker
Black-backed woodpecker
Ladder-backed woodpecker
Red-cockaded woodpecker
Nuttall's woodpecker
Strickland's woodpecker
Pileated woodpecker
Sulphur-bellied flycatcher
Great crested flycatcher*
Brown-crested flycatcher
Ash-throated flycatcher*
Dusky-capped flycatcher
Western flycatcher
Tree swallow*
Violet-green swallow*
Purple martin*
Tufted titmouse*
Plain titmouse*
Bridled titmouse
Black-capped chickadee*
Carolina chickadee*
Mexican chickadee
Mountain chickadee*
Chestnut-backed chickadee*
Siberian tit
Boreal chickadee
White-breasted nuthatch*
Red-breasted nuthatch*
Pygmy nuthatch
Brown-headed nuthatch
Brown creeper
House wren*
Winter wren
Carolina wren*
Bewick's wren*

Eastern bluebird*
Western bluebird*
Mountain bluebird*
Crested myna
Starling*
Prothonotary warbler*
Lucy's warbler
Eurasian tree sparrow
House sparrow*
House finch*

BUYING A BIRDHOUSE

Your Choice

You may buy a birdhouse or build one yourself. If you wish to take the do-it-yourself route, see the section "Constructing Birdhouses," pages 34–47. If you wish to buy one, you will have a variety of choices. Many good birdhouses are commercially available, and new houses are being introduced all the time. You can purchase birdhouses at lawn and garden, hardware, and gift stores, and through mail-order catalogs.

Below are some important criteria to consider when buying a birdhouse. Following these suggestions will ensure that the house you choose will be both functional and safe for the birds.

Criteria

THE RIGHT DIMENSIONS

Different species of birds require birdhouses of different dimensions. Check the chart on page 14 to see if the house that you are considering meets the requirements of the bird that you are trying to attract. The entrance hole should be large enough to admit the bird, but not so large as to admit unwanted species. The interior area of the house should be large enough so that the bird can build a nest sized appropriately to hold its babies, while not so large that the bird would have a difficult time filling it with nesting material. The box should be deep enough so that several inches of space will remain between the top of the nest and the entrance hole, making it more difficult for any predator to reach in and harm the babies.

If you are trying to attract a variety of backyard cavity-nesting birds, put up several boxes with different dimensions. If you have to choose one box, choose one with an entrance hole 1½ inches in diameter, because the greatest variety of birds can use such a box. For a full discussion of proper dimensions, see "What Size House?," pages 12–15.

PROPER MATERIALS

Birdhouses should be constructed of materials that have enough insulating quality to protect the birds and the eggs from excessive heat or excessive cold. Wood that is ⅝ to ¾ inch thick is a

The prothonotary warbler uses nest boxes along streams, rivers, and wetland areas. It is one of our most colorful cavity nesters.

good choice. There are also some new composite materials on the market that supposedly possess this quality. When in doubt, check with the manufacturer. Do not buy birdhouses made out of metal (although purple martin houses made of aluminum are acceptable). The box should not be constructed or stained with any materials that could be harmful to the birds, such as lead-based paint, creosote, or pressure-treated lumber.

PROPER VENTILATION

There should be good ventilation in the box, either through holes drilled near the top of the sides, or through some slit or crack at the top of the sides that lets air circulate.

DRAINAGE

There should be holes or slits in the bottom of the box so that water will drain out and not accumulate.

A WAY TO CLEAN OUT THE BOX

Preferably the top, front, or side of the box should open to make cleaning and monitoring possible.

COLOR

Birds perceive color. The colors of their plumage have subtle and complex meaning to other members of their species. Birdhouses now come in many colors and designs, and it is difficult to know how these colors affect birds. While under some circumstances birds may nest in brightly colored boxes, to ensure success it is wise to choose boxes of more muted colors that blend with the natural environment. For purple martins, white houses are acceptable; the color helps to reflect the heat.

INSIDE GROOVES

Ideally, on the inside beneath the hole there should be horizontal grooves to help the young crawl to the entrance when they are ready to fledge.

A male mountain bluebird attending the nest.

PERCHES

There is no need for a perch on a birdhouse; cavity-nesting birds do not require them. In some cases, perches might make the birdhouse more attractive to unwanted species of birds such as starlings and house sparrows.

OVERHANG

It is desirable to have the roof overhang the entrance hole by 1 to 2 inches. This protects it from rain and sun.

MOUNTING

There should be a way to hang or mount the box on a tree or post.

WHAT SIZE HOUSE?

What Size Entrance Hole?

One of the biggest controversies about birdhouses is what size box and entrance hole attracts which birds. In articles or pamphlets on birdhouses you will see many different dimensions suggested for the same bird.

How are you to know which dimensions are right for, or most attractive to, the birds? Some of the best answers are provided by taking a closer look at what these birds do in the wild. After all, what you are trying to do in putting up a birdhouse is to recreate the bird's natural nesting environment.

What Did Birds Do Before Birdhouses Were Made?

There are two kinds of cavity nesters: primary and secondary. Primary cavity nesters, such as woodpeckers and some nuthatches and chickadees, make their own tree cavities by chiseling out the wood with their bills. Secondary cavity nesters, such as wrens, titmice, swallows, bluebirds, and others, use ready-made cavities — either made by a primary cavity nester or occurring naturally in the wood through rotting or some accident to the tree.

The only birds that can really control the size of their nest holes are the primary cavity nesters. All secondary cavity nesters, which are in the majority, have to use whatever they can find.

The smallest entrance hole made by a bird is that of the downy woodpecker, and it tends to be 1¼ inches in diameter. All other holes are larger than this. Therefore, before birdhouses were made, any hole less than 1¼ inches in diameter would have been hard to find. Most birds could not be very fussy about what size hole they used for nesting. In fact, they were lucky to find *any* hole that was suitable.

What Are the Important Features of Birdhouse Entrance Holes?

Even with all that we have said above, there are still some important sizing criteria for entrance holes. The most important is that the hole must not be too small for the birds to pass through, or so tight a fit that too much feather wear occurs as they come in and out. Therefore, it is better for the hole to be a little larger than too small.

The other important feature of an entrance hole is that it be small enough to keep out the aggressive and ubiquitous starlings, which will otherwise monopolize your nest boxes to the exclusion of smaller native species. The critical dimension is a diameter of 1⁹⁄₁₆ inches. A hole any larger than this allows starlings to get in. If the entrance hole is 1⁹⁄₁₆ inches or smaller, starlings will be excluded. Of course, if you are buying or making a birdhouse for a larger bird, such as a purple martin, flicker, or kestrel, then the hole will have to be larger than 1⁹⁄₁₆ inches, and starlings may use the house.

The house sparrow is another bird that is an aggressive cavity nester and may monopolize birdhouses. In order to exclude it, the entrance hole diameter must be 1⅛ inches or smaller. The problem is that this size is too small for many more desirable nesting birds, such as bluebirds, swallows, and the larger species of titmice and chickadees. For more on house sparrows and starlings see pages 76–77.

What Size Box?

The other dimension controversy concerns the size of the interior of the box. People want to know which box size is most attractive to which species. If we remember that all secondary cavity nesters have to find a cavity already made, then

There are many important dimensions to a birdhouse, including its entrance-hole diameter and interior size.

it is easy to see that there has got to be a fair amount of leeway in what birds will accept. And, in fact, others' studies and our own surveys have shown this to be true.

There are two aspects of the interior dimensions of a birdhouse to consider. One is the size of the floor plan, and the other is the distance from the entrance hole to the bottom of the box.

Scientific studies of birds in Europe and North America have shown that smaller floor plans can cause some species of birds to lay fewer eggs in a given brood. In larger boxes, these same birds often lay more eggs. At the same time, a house that has too big a floor plan may cause more work for the birds as they try to fill it with nesting material, or it may be so big that they cannot make a properly formed nest.

The distance of the entrance hole from the bottom of the box should be great enough so the birds can build a nest 2 to 3 inches high and still have 3 to 4 inches of space from the top of the nest to the bottom of the entrance hole. This distance provides some measure of safety from predators that may try to reach into the nest box to get the eggs or young. It is also not so great that it will prevent the young birds, in the later stages of nestling life, from reaching the nest hole, looking out, and getting food when the parent lands on the front of the box.

Recommended Dimensions for Birdhouses

(All dimensions are in inches)

Bird	Entrance Hole		Floor Dimensions (Box Interior)	Total Height of Box
	Diameter	Height above floor		
Bluebirds				
Eastern	1½	6–7	4 x 4	11–12
Mountain	1⁹⁄₁₆	6–7	5½ x 5½	11–12
Western	1⁹⁄₁₆	6–7	5 x 5	11–12
Chickadees				
Black-capped	1⅛–1½	6–7	4 x 4 to 5 x 5	9–12
Carolina	1⅛–1½	6–7	4 x 4 to 5 x 5	9–12
Chestnut-backed	1⅛–1½	6–7	4 x 4 to 5 x 5	9–12
Mountain	1⅛–1½	6–7	4 x 4 to 5 x 5	9–12
Ducks				
Barrow's goldeneye	3½ x 4½	16–18	10 x 10 to 12 x 12	24–25
Bufflehead	2½–3	17–19	6 x 6 to 7 x 7	17–19
Common goldeneye	3½ x 4½	16–18	10 x 10 to 12 x 12	24–25
Common merganser	4 x 5	16–18	10 x 10 to 12 x 12	24–25
Hooded merganser	3 x 4	16–18	10 x 10 to 12 x 12	24–25
Wood duck	3 x 4	16–18	10 x 10 to 12 x 12	24–25
Finch				
House	1⅜–2	5–7	4 x 4 to 5 x 5	9–12
Flycatchers				
Ash-throated	1½–2½	6–7	5 x 5 to 6 x 6	9–12
Great crested	1½–2½	6–7	5 x 5 to 6 x 6	9–12
Kestrel				
American	3	10–12	8 x 8 to 9 x 9	14–16
Martin				
Purple	2–2½	1	6 x 6	6
Nuthatches				
Red-breasted	1⅛–1½	6–7	4 x 4 to 5 x 5	9–12
White-breasted	1⅛–1½	6–7	4 x 4 to 5 x 5	9–12
Owls				
Barred	6–8	14–18	13 x 13 to 14 x 14	22–28
Common barn	6–8	4	16 wide, 22 deep	16
Northern saw-whet	2½–4	10–12	6 x 6 to 8 x 8	15–18
Screech	2½–4	10–12	6 x 6 to 8 x 8	15–18
Sparrow				
House	1³⁄₁₆–2	6–7	4 x 4 to 5 x 5	9–12
Starling				
European	1⅝–4	6–10	5 x 5 to 6 x 6	13–20
Swallows				
Tree	1¼–1½	6–7	4 x 4 to 5 x 5	9–12
Violet-green	1¼–1½	6–7	4 x 4 to 5 x 5	9–12
Titmice				
Plain	1⅜–1½	6–7	4 x 4 to 5 x 5	9–12
Tufted	1⅜–1½	6–7	4 x 4 to 5 x 5	9–12
Warbler				
Prothonotary	1¼–1½	5–7	4 x 4 to 5 x 5	9–12
Woodpeckers				
Downy	1¼–1½	8–12	3 x 3 to 4 x 4	10–14
Hairy	1¾–2¾	10–14	5 x 5 to 6 x 6	14–16
Northern flicker	2–3	10–20	6 x 6 to 8 x 8	14–24
Red-bellied	1¾–2¾	10–14	5 x 5 to 6 x 6	14–16
Red-headed	1¾–2¾	10–14	5 x 5 to 6 x 6	14–16
Wrens				
Bewick's	1¼–1½	6–7	4 x 4 to 5 x 5	9–12
Carolina	1½	6–7	4 x 4 to 5 x 5	9–12
House	1–1½	6–7	4 x 4 to 5 x 5	9–12

A primary cavity nester at work. This red-bellied woodpecker male is tossing chips from his new nest hole. The fungus at the top of the picture shows that this wood has probably already been softened through the growth of the fungus.

Recommendations

The recommendations for birdhouse dimensions listed on the accompanying chart are based on a thorough knowledge of the birds and their behavior in the wild, as well as surveys — our own and others' — and extensive experience with birdhouses of all makes and sizes.

What we have tried to provide is an easy set of guidelines. We have given a range of dimensions wherever possible. This is, again, in keeping with our knowledge of the great variety of circumstances birds will accept in the wild.

The upper limit for entrance-hole sizes has been kept to 1½ inches for the smaller birds, even though many of them will accept larger dimensions. This is because this dimension excludes starlings. With many of the smaller birds, such as chickadees, wrens, nuthatches, and titmice, our experience is that they often prefer the larger

of the dimensions listed. In fact, a hole size of 1½ inches is attractive to all of them and is probably the most popular all-around hole size that still keeps out starlings. See "A Super Easy Birdhouse," page 38.

More detailed information on each species' birdhouse requirements is provided with their life history descriptions in the second half of the book and in the chart on the facing page.

More Than Just Dimensions

Some people get so absorbed in birdhouse dimensions that they forget about other factors critical to attracting cavity nesters. Remember that you must be in an area of the country where the bird breeds and also have its favored habitat on your property in order to attract it. Range maps for each species and their favored habitats are listed in the individual species accounts.

PUTTING UP YOUR BIRDHOUSE

Where

Once you have either bought or made a birdhouse, the next question is where to put it. The first consideration is that the house be placed in the right habitat for the bird you are trying to attract. For example, chickadees nest in wooded areas and bluebirds nest in open areas. Do not expect to attract bluebirds in the middle of the woods or chickadees in the middle of a field.

Most suburban properties that have a good mixture of trees, shrubs, and some lawn can attract a wide variety of birds. Refer to the species accounts to determine which birds will be attracted to your property.

If you want to attract some of the woodland species, try to place the box within 10 to 15 feet of a shrub that can serve as a perch for the birds as they come to and go from the house. Birds often like to stop and look around to be sure the coast is clear before they enter the birdhouse. Also, if one parent is in the box feeding the young, the other parent has a convenient place to wait until the other leaves.

Another placement consideration is, will you be able to see the birdhouse easily so that you can enjoy the birds' breeding behavior? Remember, birdhouses are also for your own pleasure.

When to Put It Up

The best time of year to put up a birdhouse is late winter or early spring, when birds arrive at their breeding ground and begin to search for suitable nesting spots.

For birds that are year-round residents, such as chickadees, titmice, or nuthatches, fall and winter are also good times. The birds will explore the houses in these seasons and may use them to roost in at night. The following spring they may then go on to use them as nest sites as well.

Mounting the Box

Birdhouses need to be attached to a support. Trees are good places to mount them. You can use screws or nails. With screws, you can loosen the attachment a little bit each year to allow for the growth of the tree. Many boxes also can be mounted on poles or posts.

If you mount the birdhouse on a fence post near livestock, make sure it is on the opposite side from the livestock so that they cannot jar or dislodge the box as they try to scratch themselves.

Suspension from wires can work well for a smaller birdhouse, such as one for wrens. Hang it from two wires secured to either end of the house to prevent it from twirling around.

For birds that are particularly tolerant of humans, such as wrens or house finches, the birdhouse may be mounted on your house or on an outbuilding, such as a barn or shed.

How High

In the species accounts, we give a range of heights at which you can place birdhouses for particular birds. It is important to keep in mind that there is no exact right or wrong height for most of these birds. In the wild they would have to accept whatever cavity or suitable excavation spot they could find. Most of the birds discussed in this book will accept birdhouses placed from 5 to 50 feet high. Probably the best recommendation is to place the house at a height that you can reach, since you are the one who will be doing the monitoring and cleaning out of the box.

What Direction

It is preferable to place the birdhouse so that it faces away from the prevailing winds, to prevent rain from blowing in. Generally this means

A mountain bluebird perched on a tree stump.

mounting the box to face south or east. If this is not feasible, mount the box in whatever direction you want. We have seen most of the smaller cavity-nesting birds use houses that face in any direction. In a scientific study of the importance of 10 cavity variables to cavity-nesting birds, the volume of the cavity was determined to be more important than any other factor, including the compass orientation of the entrance hole.

When Will Birds Use It?

It is hard to predict just when a bird will use a birdhouse, since there are many factors that affect this, such as how many cavity nesters are on your property, what natural cavities are available, and even the age of the birdhouse (birds often prefer older houses).

We have had birds use boxes within days of our putting them up; in other cases, it has taken several years for a birdhouse to be occupied. If a house is not used within two years, change its location and you might have better luck.

How Many Birdhouses Should I Put Up?

There is no limit to the number of birdhouses that you can put up on your property, but there is a limit to the number that will be used by the birds. This limit is determined by the habitat and ter-

ritorial needs of each species. If you have only open fields or dense woods, then you will attract only the species that prefer these habitats. In general, the more habitats you have, the more birds you will be able to attract.

The territorial behavior of each species also will limit the number of pairs that will use your nest boxes. For example, chickadees tend to have breeding territories of about 10 acres, and within that area they will not allow any other chickadees to breed. Thus, you are unlikely to have more than one pair of chickadees on your property if it is less than 10 acres, unless your property overlaps two chickadee territories. On the other hand, the chickadees will not keep out other cavity nesters, such as titmice or wrens, that might nest in the same habitat.

For other birds, such as tree swallows, that do not defend large territories, many pairs may nest in the same small area. Thus, in our 2-acre field we have 14 birdhouses that are used primarily by tree swallows. In our woods we have about 5 birdhouses per acre. Even though we provide all of these houses, only about half of them are used each year. Many other birds nest in the natural cavities that we try to keep in our woods.

In the species accounts we have listed the habitat requirements and the territory size for each bird to help you determine how many birds of each species may nest on your property and, in turn, how many birdhouses to put up.

FAMILY LIFE

The Real Reward

Gaining an intimate glimpse of the family life of birds is the real reward for having put up a birdhouse. Wondrous and special moments will occur as you watch the birds raise their young. In order to enrich your experience and help you to interpret what you see, here is a generalized account of what takes place during the breeding cycle of a cavity-nesting bird.

A black-capped chickadee inspecting a box as a possible breeding site.

Setting Up a Territory

The changing light levels of late winter and early spring affect birds' hormones and trigger breeding behavior. Males sing and defend a territory from other males as they try to attract mates. Females select and pair with male birds. Often a male's territory includes one or several good nest cavities; if you are lucky, it may include one of your birdhouses.

Choosing a Birdhouse

One or both birds will investigate the birdhouse by landing on it, cautiously peering in, and then going inside. This investigating may occur over a period of days or weeks and may include several houses or cavities before one is chosen. We remember the day a male bluebird showed up on our property. We followed him around for the whole morning, watching him investigate at least 10 different birdhouses, a few tree cavities, and our neighbor's lamppost, which was minus the lamp at the time and consisted of a hollow 4-inch-diameter pipe. We watched him land and peer inside, fearing he would fall in, but he didn't. The next day he returned with a female and tried to interest her in at least 5 different houses by flying to them and singing to her.

Nest Building

A good sign that a pair is serious about a birdhouse is when the female starts to bring in nesting material. Even at this stage of the game, she may switch houses. We had a titmouse start to build a nest in one box and then switch to another. Then a wren moved into the house the titmouse had abandoned. Generally, though, once nest building begins it continues in the same birdhouse.

Two black-capped chick-adees, probably a mated pair, may be thinking of excavating at the end of this birch stub. Chick-adees often excavate in the rotted wood of dead birches.

Nest building takes place most frequently in the morning. The male usually guards the birdhouse while the female makes trips to gather nesting material, or he may follow her around. Some males may add a little material, but it is usually the female that builds the nest. Interestingly, in the case of the house wren, the male builds several partial nests; the female chooses one, and adds a lining.

Egg Laying

When the nest is complete, egg laying may begin immediately, or the birds may wait several days or longer. During this interval the birds will mate. This is quite easy to watch in some of the species that nest in open habitats, like tree swallows and bluebirds. Tree swallows often mate on top of the birdhouse. To mate, the male lands on the female's back, and she lifts her tail up while he bends his tail down. Their cloacas touch and sperm is transferred.

Eggs are laid usually in the early morning, one per day, until the clutch is complete. Clutch size varies with the species; to find this information look under each species account. During this period, the birds go near the box only when the female lays an egg. The rest of the time they stay away — but do not think that they have abandoned the nest.

Incubation

When the last egg is laid, the female will begin incubating. She sits on the eggs constantly, taking breaks only to get food, stretch, and preen. In

A female mountain bluebird incubating eggs. She will not move, even though the birdhouse is open and a picture is being taken.

Mountain bluebird eggs and nestlings at the moment of hatching. The dark streaks are actually wet down.

some species, like titmice and bluebirds, the male may bring food to the female at the box. When the female is out feeding, the male may enter the box and guard it. In a few species, notably woodpeckers and owls, both sexes take turns incubating.

Nestling Phase

The eggs hatch over a period of a day or two; however, there are few outward clues to its occurrence. Your best clue to the onset of this phase is seeing the parents bringing food to the nest. They will make many trips, and it soon keeps both of them quite busy, leaving them barely enough time to take breaks and find food for themselves.

At first the nestlings' eyes are closed, and they barely make a sound. They will raise their heads if the box is jiggled by the landing of a parent, or if you open it. They are tiny and naked except for a few down feathers. They cannot regulate their own body heat, so the female sits over them, brooding them to keep them warm. She leaves briefly to get food. The male may bring food to the nest and pass it to the female, who then feeds it to the babies.

Mountain bluebirds in the early days of the nestling phase. They have practically no feathers and still need their mother's brooding to keep them warm.

A female eastern bluebird bringing food to the nestlings. It's a good possibility that when she leaves, she will be carrying away a fecal sac.

The young grow rapidly. After several days their eyes open, they are covered with downy feathers, and they make peeping sounds when fed. Toward the end of the nestling phase the young have grown quite large, are fully feathered, and make loud, begging noises when parents arrive with food. When you open the house to see them, they react by cowering down and remaining silent.

The parents carry out fecal sacs from the nest — nature's system of nest sanitation. A fecal sac contains the baby's excreta in a tidy white membrane. At the very end of the nestling phase the young excrete on the rim of the nest, and the nest becomes soiled. By then it does not matter, since they are just about to leave.

Nestling life lasts about 2 to 3 weeks for birds that nest in birdhouses. Instinctively, they know when to leave. One by one they exit over a period of hours, or in some cases a day or two. They can fly quite well, better than their counterparts in open-cup nests.

Fledgling Phase

Young that have left the nest but are still fed by the parents are called fledglings. This stage lasts

Mountain bluebirds in the later part of the nestling phase. They have all of their feathers at this point, but their wings and tails still have to grow longer.

Two eastern bluebirds in the fledging stage. They are still being fed by the parents now, but fairly soon they will have to fend for themselves.

several weeks or more, depending on the species. If the parents begin another brood, the fledgling stage may be shortened, or the male might take care of the first brood while the female is busy with nesting duties. The fledglings generally do not go back into the box once they leave, but wander about a great deal; they may move out of your yard. They still beg noisily and may fly after the parents in hot pursuit or sit in one spot and constantly call. The harried parents eventually stop feeding the fledglings and may even become aggressive toward them. By this time, the young have learned to find food for themselves. They then usually disperse or migrate.

Renesting

Renestings may occur after a successful first brood, or they may occur if the first attempt is unsuccessful. Many birds keep trying to raise young throughout a season, even after one or two unsuccessful attempts. Birds may or may not use the same box for subsequent broods.

MONITORING AND KEEPING NEST RECORDS

How to Monitor

Birdhouses should be monitored or checked regularly. This can be both rewarding and educational for you, and it helps to ensure the health and safety of the birds.

It is *not* true that visiting or touching a bird's nest will make the adults desert the nest. Most birds have a very poor sense of smell, and even when they see you visit the nest, they will return within minutes of your leaving.

Approach the birdhouse in a normal manner and quietly open it. Sometimes we first tap on the box, giving any adult bird inside the opportunity to leave before we open it. On occasion, we have had tree swallows and bluebirds calmly remain in the box incubating eggs, in which case we close the box and leave them undisturbed.

A young bluebird being checked for its health during an experienced monitor's visit. It is a myth that parent birds will abandon their young if the birdhouse or the young have been touched by humans.

When to Monitor

During the nesting season, monitor your birdhouses at least once a week. You should not monitor the boxes in bad weather, or when the nestlings are within 4 days of leaving the nest, as this may cause them to leave before they are ready. Check the length of the nestling phase for each bird in the species accounts so that you will know when the birds will be leaving the birdhouse. When in doubt, don't monitor.

Keeping Records

We find it fun to keep a record of the nesting progress at each of our birdhouses. We have provided a sample nest record card on page 95, which you may copy. Ask yourself: Is the nest complete? How many eggs or young are there? How old are the young? Very young birds have almost no feathers, just a little down covering, and they may lift their heads and gape when the nest is touched. Slightly older nestlings have feathers that are growing in sheaths that look like quills. Still older nestlings have feathers that have broken out of the sheaths; the birds will cower down in the nest when the birdhouse is opened.

When Problems Arise

Watching nesting birds successfully raise a brood can be a great joy, and in the majority of cases everything goes smoothly. Occasionally, however, problems occur. It is best to know in advance what these might be and how to deal with them effectively.

If you find dead adults or young, or if you think the young have disappeared because of predation (rather than simply because it was time for them to fledge), you might feel upset. This is understandable. But do not feel guilty, and remember that similar things occur in nature all the time.

Nest identification

Knowing these 5 common nests will help you to understand and record what has happened in your birdhouses. These houses were opened up after the breeding season for this picture. Here are some clues to identifying each species' nest. Chickadee or titmouse: moss, fur, and other downy materials. House sparrow: feathers mixed into a jumble of grasses, cloth, and other odds and ends. Eastern bluebird: a nicely made nest of grasses and no other materials. Tree swallow: a nest of grasses that is just lined with feathers. House wren: a nest of solid twigs, sometimes lined with finer fibers.

By providing safe nest boxes and monitoring them, you are most probably helping the birds to have greater nesting success than they might ordinarily have on their own.

Remove any dead birds from the nest. If all the nestlings have perished, clean out the nesting material; this gives the parents a chance to renest. The urge to reproduce in birds is strong, and most birds will continue to try to raise young and renest if a disaster befalls their previous attempt. Often, however, they will make a new nest in a different spot. This is why it is preferable to have more than one box available.

Do not attempt to raise young birds yourself; it is against the law. Nestlings can be considered to be abandoned only if you know that both parents have died, or if the young seem extremely weak. If that is the case, contact your local Audubon Society or wild bird rehabilitation center. They are better equipped than you can be to handle the situation.

If you suspect predation on a nest, take steps to predator-proof the birdhouse for the next occupant. See the following chapter, "Controlling Predators and Competitors."

Maintenance

Clean out each birdhouse after each nesting and again in early spring. This prevents a buildup of mites and other parasites. We use an old pancake spatula and a stiff paintbrush to make this job easier. If your houses are exceptionally soiled, you may want to wash them out with soap; rinse thoroughly. Repair or replace any boxes that need it before next spring. Some people prefer to plug up the holes of the boxes during the winter to prevent mice from using them or to deter starlings or house sparrows, who often become attached to a box and start adding nest material in winter. Unplug holes in early spring when the other birds start looking for nest sites.

CONTROLLING PREDATORS AND COMPETITORS

A Limited Resource

Since tree holes are a limited resource, there is sometimes fierce competition for them among cavity nesters. We have seen bluebirds usurp the birdhouse of tree swallows, and vice versa; tree swallows oust titmice; and house wrens take over a swallow nest. Birds of the same species also compete with one another.

A raccoon emerging from a resting spot. Raccoons can prey on birds' nests.

To lessen competition and meet the demand for nesting sites, it is a good idea to put up several birdhouses of different sizes on your property. You may also have to take additional steps to control predators and competitors.

House Sparrows and Starlings

House sparrows and starlings are aggressive, imported species that nest in holes in man-made structures, natural cavities, and birdhouses. They are the main competitors with native cavity-nesting birds. Since they are an introduced species, they (and pigeons) are not protected by law, as are our native birds. It is legal to trap and remove house sparrows and starlings.

Starlings can be excluded from birdhouses with entrance holes 1½ inches or less in diameter, since these are too small for them to enter. If you have put up birdhouses with larger entrance holes, and starlings are attracted, repeatedly remove their nesting material, or, if necessary, trap and remove the birds.

House sparrows are more of a problem, because they will nest in any bird box with an entrance hole larger than 1⅛ inches in diameter. While no one yet, to our knowledge, has invented a bird box that is shunned by house sparrows, there are ways to control these birds. Since some house sparrows may claim birdhouses in winter, it is a good idea to keep birdhouse entrances plugged up until spring, so the birds do not get a head start on migrant and other native nesting species. We have also had success in deterring house sparrows by repeatedly removing their nesting material. This may require perseverance, since they may continue to try renesting for weeks.

Placing boxes in habitats that house sparrows

do not frequent is another good solution. For example, house sparrows rarely nest in deep woods or rural areas a mile or more from farm buildings.

In some cases, when house sparrows are a persistent problem, they may have to be trapped and removed. You must trap the male house sparrow, because if only the female is removed, the male will remain attached to the site and get a new mate.

There are traps for a single box that work by shutting off the hole when the bird is in the box. There are also traps for catching larger numbers of birds. Information on traps is available from the sources listed in "Resources." Extreme care should be taken when using any trap to be sure no native species of bird is caught or harmed, since they, as noted, are protected by law.

Raccoons

One of the most common predators that visit birdhouses is raccoons. Signs of raccoon predation include nesting material pulled from a box and claw marks on the box. Birdhouses that are mounted on metal poles are most easily raccoon-proofed. Coat the pole with a very thick layer of automobile or marine grease (available from automotive or marine supply stores). One application in spring should last the season, but it may have to be repeated. In addition, attach a 2-foot length of 4- or 5-inch-diameter stovepipe or PVC pipe around the pole under the birdhouse. A raccoon will not be able to get a claw hold on the smooth surface. Another effective baffle is a 36-inch-diameter metal cone or "skirt" attached to the pole directly below the birdhouse, open end down.

To protect birdhouses mounted on trees, put a 3-foot-wide strip of galvanized metal around the tree (painted brown for better appearance if you wish). Secure it with nails but maintain a loose fit all around to allow for air circulation and growth of the tree. Make sure the birdhouse is on a lone tree whose canopy does not connect with those of other trees, so raccoons cannot gain access by climbing over from the other trees.

Some people put a baffle over the birdhouse entrance, often using a ¾-inch-thick block of wood with a hole in its middle the same size as

Tree swallow at nest box. In open areas, tree swallows are competing with bluebirds, house wrens, house sparrows, and starlings for nest boxes.

the entrance hole. This may make it more difficult for predators to reach down into the nest.

Devices that extend out from the entrance hole farther — at least 3 inches or more — are probably even more effective. Such devices include a plastic tube, sold commercially, that snaps onto the entrance hole, and the Noel nest guard — a rectangular hardware cloth sleeve that is stapled around the entrance hole (see diagram for how to construct this). The birds, however, must learn to go through these to reach the entrance hole of the

A white-footed mouse peering out of a knot-hole. These mice like to occupy birdhouses for a few weeks at a time, especially in winter.

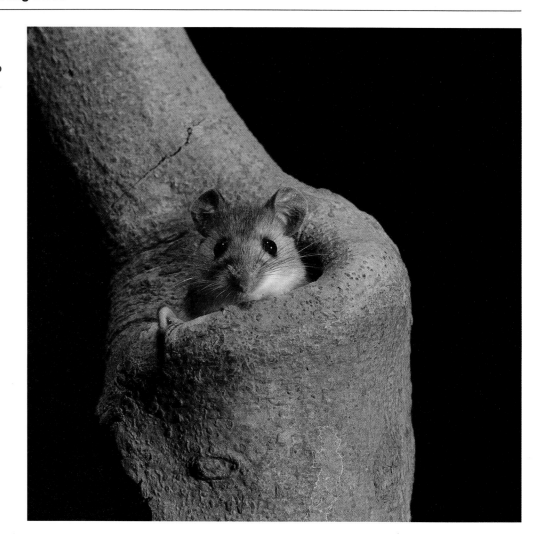

box, and not all birds will accept these devices. You may have to experiment to see which works in your situation. Our experience has been that these extended devices are best accepted by a bird after it has already chosen the birdhouse, when it is in the nest-building stage of breeding or beyond.

Other Predators and Competitors

Aside from raccoons, the other major predators of birds who nest in birdhouses are cats and snakes. Cats can be deterred from climbing up to boxes by the use of the predator guards mentioned above. Since cats are often more of a problem once fledglings have left the nest, it is wise to keep your cat confined indoors until fledglings are self-sufficient or until they have left the area.

In many areas of the country, although less so in the Northeast, snakes are a problem. To deter them, mount the birdhouse on a metal pole that is covered with a 5-foot-high section of 4-inch-diameter smooth PVC pipe and spread several shovelfuls of sharp sand (masonry or concrete) around the base of the PVC pipe. An effective live snake trap, the Kruegar snake trap, is made out of the kind of mesh netting used to keep birds from eating berry crops. The mesh is fashioned into a skirt that surrounds the mounting pole or post. For further information, see "Resources."

Squirrels occasionally chew at and enlarge the entrances of birdhouses and may eat the eggs. Reinforcing the hole with a wooden block or metal plate placed over it will deter squirrels from chewing. Small mice can eat bird eggs, but mice seem to be more interested in taking over the birdhouse to live in themselves, especially in the winter. During spring cleaning of houses, remove any mice nests. (The mice themselves gen-

Predator Baffles

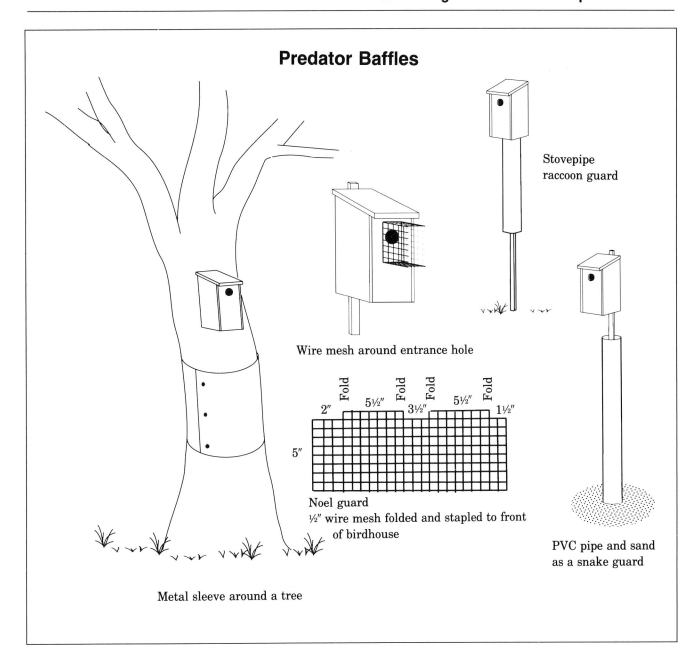

Stovepipe raccoon guard

Wire mesh around entrance hole

Noel guard
½" wire mesh folded and stapled to front of birdhouse

PVC pipe and sand as a snake guard

Metal sleeve around a tree

erally jump out of the box when it is opened.) The mice will rarely return.

Ants and wasps may build their nests in birdhouses and prevent the birds from using them. Control them by spraying with pyrethrum, a spray harmless to birds that is available at garden stores. As an alternative, some people dissuade wasps from building in a birdhouse by putting a thin layer of Vaseline on the ceiling of the house. In the South, fire ants may be controlled by putting Tanglefoot, a sticky substance available at garden stores, around the mounting pole.

Blowflies are a species of fly whose young or larvae (which are small, grayish, and ⅜ inch large or less) live in birds' nests and at night feed on the blood of the nestlings. During the day, the larvae hide deep in the nesting material. Blowflies are often found in bluebird and tree swallow nests. Check the nest by lifting it slightly and tapping it, always being careful of the nestlings. Scrape the chaff from under the nest into your hand. If you discover blowfly larvae, remove the infested nesting material and fashion a new nest for the nestlings out of clean, dry grass.

ATTRACTING OTHER NESTING BIRDS

Other Nesting Sites

Besides cavities, there are three main places that birds nest: in shrubs or trees, on the ground, and in the ground. Among all the species of birds in the world, ground nesting is the most common, followed by nesting in shrubs and trees, then nesting in cavities, and finally nesting in the ground. Practically no backyard birds nest in the ground, but you may encounter and may want to provide for the other three.

Providing Ground-Nesting Sites

Some of the common birds that nest on the ground include towhees, many sparrows, meadowlarks, pheasants, many ducks, killdeer, juncos, and woodcocks. Each of these birds needs a different type of ground cover for its nesting.

Some birds, like the bobolink, meadowlark, and pheasant, need large areas of tall grasses. Most of these will be attracted only to a spot with several acres of meadow.

Other birds, like sparrows and juncos, may nest in any small clearing where there are a few tufts of grass in which to hide their nests. They would be happy with a corner of a lawn where the grass is left to grow high.

Many ducks, such as the mallard, as well as towhees and woodcocks, prefer to nest among the open understory of woods, often hiding their nests under the lowest boughs of small trees or blending them in with the fallen, dried leaf litter.

And, finally, the killdeer prefers to be right out in the open with practically no vegetation around at all. It is often attracted to gravel driveways, rocky areas with sparse vegetation, and even flat rooftops.

Thus, in providing habitats for any number of these birds you may need to cultivate a variety of ground vegetation and cover.

Providing Shrub- and Tree-Nesting Sites

Shrubs are one of the most important elements in attracting birds to nest. They not only provide good sites for nests at a height convenient for the birds, but also produce berries and attract insects on which the birds can feed.

Many shrubs tend to grow in or at the edge of more open areas. This creates what has been called the "edge effect." Wildlife, and birds in particular, are attracted to edge environments because they present the greatest variety of habitats. Creating dense shrub edges at the borders of your lawn, a field, or woods is the best way to attract birds.

Trees are also important, but are best when interspersed with open areas and shrubs. Alone, a forest of tall trees will attract very few birds and is a kind of desert for wildlife. The leaf canopy is high, often there is little growth beneath owing to lack of light, and thus the amounts of food, cover, and nesting areas are inadequate.

When deciding on trees to attract birds, choose a variety of sizes and types. Try to have some smaller trees — crab apples, dogwoods, hawthorns — as well as taller trees — maples, cherries, oaks, and ashes. Have evergreens for added cover and protection of nesting or roosting birds, and deciduous trees for good perches. Include trees that produce a variety of foods, such as fruits, seeds, nuts, and cones.

Platform Nesters

There are several common backyard birds that can be attracted to nest on or in buildings if a small shelf or platform is provided. These include the American robin, barn swallow, eastern phoebe, black phoebe, and Say's phoebe. Occa-

A male robin — one of the birds, along with some phoebes and some swallows, that can be attracted by putting up a small platform.

sionally cave and cliff swallows may also be attracted to platforms.

Each of these can be found nesting on naturally occurring shelflike projections of buildings, especially if these places are under an eave or are otherwise protected from rain. These spots include barn rafters, the tops of front porch lights, roof gutters, and windowsills. By building a small shelf or platform and attaching it to the side of a building or inside an open garage or barn, you can duplicate the sort of nesting site these birds find attractive.

Of these birds, the robin is the most flexible and would just as soon build its nest in a shrub or tree as on a building. The phoebes often nest near water, under bridges or docks, for example, but they are happy on houses as well and generally are not disturbed by human comings and goings. The barn swallow is partial to the interiors of large, open buildings, such as warehouses or barns, although we know of a pair nesting in a neighbor's garage.

For a plan for a nesting platform, see "Advanced Birdhouse Plans," page 45.

Providing Nesting Materials

Each species of bird uses slightly different materials to make its nest. Often, these materials can be in short supply. Therefore, it is good to provide the birds with a variety of nesting materials. One easy way to do this is by stuffing a suet holder with fur, feathers, short bits of string, strands of cloth, or bits of cellophane. All of these materials are attractive to certain birds. Some people just stuff a string bag with nesting materials.

The suet holder or string bag should be hung where the birds can see it plainly. You can attach it to the top of a pole that you put up in the middle of your lawn.

Another nesting material that many birds use is mud. Choose a part of your yard at nesting season, keep it clear of vegetation, and water it

Where Other Backyard Birds Nest

On the Ground	(In Shrubs, cont.)	In Trees	On Platforms
Canada goose	Common yellowthroat	Red-tailed hawk	Eastern phoebe
Mallard	Rose-breasted grosbeak	Inca dove	Black phoebe
American black duck	Northern cardinal	Mourning dove	Say's phoebe
Killdeer	Indigo bunting	Great horned owl	Cliff swallow
American woodcock	Brown towhee	Eastern wood pewee	Barn swallow
Bobwhite	Song sparrow	Western wood pewee	American robin
California quail	Chipping sparrow	Blue jay	
Ring-necked pheasant	White-crowned sparrow	American crow	
Common ground dove	Red-winged blackbird	Northwestern crow	
Rufous-sided towhee		Cedar Waxwing	
White-throated sparrow	**In Shrubs or Trees**	Common grackle	
Bobolink		Great-tailed grackle	
Western meadowlark	Yellow-billed cuckoo	Orchard oriole	
Eastern meadowlark	Black-billed cuckoo	Northern oriole	
	Eastern kingbird	Hooded oriole	
In Shrubs	Western kingbird	Scarlet tanager	
	Black-billed magpie	Western tanager	
Gray catbird	Wood thrush	Summer tanager	
Northern mockingbird	American robin	Pine siskin	
Brown thrasher	Red-eyed vireo	Lesser goldfinch	
California thrasher	Brewer's blackbird	Purple finch	
Yellow warbler			

enough to maintain a constant supply of mud. You may attract robins, barn swallows, or phoebes.

Providing Water

Water, along with food, shelter, and a proper site, is one of the main ingredients of an ideal nesting habitat. Water is easy to provide; all you need is a small pool, birdbath, or shallow dish placed in such a way that the birds will feel comfortable using it.

In our experience, birds prefer water found in open areas where they can spot any potential danger. They also like to have some perches in the open nearby from which they can look over the water area before they make their final approach. We often put our birdbaths in the lawn, at the edge of our deck, or near our bird feeders. We always cut off a branch of a shrub or tree and either stick it in the ground or attach it to a stake so that it forms a good perching site right next to the water.

Another important feature of a water area is that it have varying levels of shallow water in which the birds can bathe. Each species of bird bathes slightly differently and, depending on its size, may need water from only a half inch to several inches deep. In our birdbaths and water areas we always place several flat stones around the edge, so that the birds can gradually work their way into the water.

How Long Will It Take to Get Other Nesting Birds?

You may want to know how soon the birds will start nesting, once you create a good habitat. To answer this question, we must explain how birds choose nesting sites. Older birds that have already nested in previous years usually return to

A male northern cardinal — one of the most brightly colored backyard birds that you can attract.

the same areas to nest again. Therefore, they will not suddenly come into your yard.

This means that it is most likely that young birds that have not nested before will first have to discover your property and then decide that it is a good place in which to nest. If this happens in the first year, consider yourself lucky. More likely what will happen is that as you continually improve your property, pairs of nesting birds will gradually move in and set up nesting territories. Once they start nesting there, it is very likely that they will continue to do so year after year.

Your results with birdhouses can be much more immediate, since there are often not enough cavities to cover the demand, and even older birds need new cavities since previous ones may have decayed. Therefore, you may get birds using your birdhouses in the very first breeding season.

HOW TO BUILD A BIRDHOUSE

Why Build a Birdhouse?

Although you can buy excellent birdhouses, there are many good reasons to make one. Building a birdhouse can be fun and rewarding, and it may save you money.

Many people decide to make the building of a birdhouse a family project or to share it with children in organized groups such as scouts, camps, or school classrooms. In this chapter we will tell you all that you need to know to build a birdhouse successfully.

What You Need to Get Started

To build a birdhouse you will need a plan, several tools, various fasteners, and wood. An easy, life-size plan is presented in the following chapter, and your other needs are detailed below.

Tools and Fasteners

A word about tools. If you are just starting out with woodworking, then you probably do not have power tools. This is okay, for you can make our super easy birdhouse with just hand tools (see page 38). If you need to buy some hand tools, be sure to ask the salesperson for good quality tools. Good tools can be used on future projects and make your job easier. Cheap tools can be hard to use and soon fall apart.

SAW

Although you can make a birdhouse with a handsaw, you can do the job better by cutting out the wood with a power saw. There are various types of power saws, but those most effective for straight cuts, as are needed in building a birdhouse, are circular saws, so named because of their round blades. These are available either as hand-held models or mounted on a metal table (and thus called table saws).

DRILL

You will also need a drill. A small, hand-held, electric one will work well. It should hold a drill bit up to ⅜ inch in diameter at its base. In carpentry terms, the bit is the piece that actually drills into the wood, while the drill is the thing that holds (and drives) the bit. A large hand drill called a brace can also be used for drilling the entrance holes to birdhouses.

A birdhouse mounted on a metal garden pole. This is an easy way to put a birdhouse wherever you want it.

Tools needed to make a birdhouse. Counterclockwise, from left to right: handsaw, claw hammer, screwdriver, adjustable bit, brace, electric drill, ⅛-inch bit, ¼-inch bit, and drill saw for making entrance holes.

DRILL BIT

Since the entrance hole recommended for most birdhouses is 1½ inches in diameter, you will need a 1½-inch wood-boring bit. It has a large, flat end and a thin shank of about ¼ inch in diameter that will fit into your drill. There is also a bit called a drill saw. It is a cylinder with saw teeth at one end and is designed for cutting large holes. There are finally adjustable drill bits that enable you to drill holes of various sizes. You will also need ¼- and ⅛-inch drill bits for making ventilation and fastener holes.

HAMMER

You need a hammer with a *claw* on the back of the head that enables you to remove nails if necessary. Do not get too light a hammer, thinking that it will be easier to use; it is easier to drive a nail straight in with a heavier hammer.

SCREWDRIVER

You can use either a standard screwdriver or a Phillips screwdriver (which has a little cross at the tip). Just be sure to match the screws with the screwdriver.

NAILS OR SCREWS

You will need nails or screws to fasten the boards of your birdhouse together. There are many sizes and shapes of nails available — each one is designed to serve a slightly different purpose. The style of nail that you should use is called a *finishing* nail. Such a nail has a head only slightly larger than the diameter of the nail. The nails should also be *steel* (not aluminum) and *galvanized* — a process that keeps them from rusting.

Finally, you need to specify the length of the nail. In hardware terms, lengths are referred to as two-penny, four-penny, six-penny, etc. This is written as 2d, 4d, 6d (d stands for penny in England, where this measurement system started). For birdhouse building you will need 6d or 8d galvanized finishing nails.

You can also use wood screws. They are a little more difficult to work with, but do a better job of holding the birdhouse together. They should be thin and about 1¼ to 1½ inches long.

FASTENER

And lastly, you will need a small fastener. The side or the top of the box is built to swing open for monitoring and cleaning out of the nest. The fastener keeps the swinging side or top closed at all other times. Any kind of fastener will do.

Choosing Wood

Various types of wood can be used to build birdhouses, including plywood, redwood, red cedar, western red cedar, or pine. Plywood is the longest-lasting wood. It should be ¾ inch thick and what is termed *exterior* plywood, which holds up under exposure to rain and sun. The difficulties associated with plywood are that it is sold in large sheets, often 8 feet by 4 feet, and that it splinters, especially when cut with a handsaw.

Among other woods, redwood and cedars are good because they resist rotting. Red cedar and western red cedar are good substitutes for redwood, but these woods are not always available in all regions of the country. This leaves pine as the best and most accessible wood after plywood. Pine is not that expensive and is easy to cut and fasten.

This birdhouse placed on the trunk of a red cedar and near woods is ideal for many cavity-nesting birds, including chickadees, titmice, and nuthatches.

Lumber Lingo

When you go to buy lumber, it is helpful to know how it is measured and how its quality is evaluated. Here is a brief guide to "lumber lingo."

When referring to the size of a board, you say the thickness and width first — thus a "two-by-four" (2 x 4) is 2 inches thick by 4 inches wide; a "one-by-eight" (1 x 8) is 1 inch thick and 8 inches wide. You will build birdhouses out of wood that is 1 inch thick and 4 to 8 inches wide. You then must specify the length of the board, such as a two-by-four, 8 feet long.

The thickness and width of a board, however, are measured when the board is first rough-cut. The boards are then planed or smoothed, which means they are slightly thinner and narrower when you buy them. Thus, all boards called 1 inch thick are actually ¾ inch thick; a 10-inch-wide board is actually only 9¼ inches wide. The lengths of boards are accurate.

Finally, when buying lumber, you will be asked what grade you want. With pine, the grade refers to how many knots are in the wood. The more knots, the less valuable and the less expensive. The best grade is often referred to as *select, d-select,* or sometimes *clear* pine. This can be very expensive. The next best grade is often called *common* pine. This is fine for birdhouses and will help you keep your costs down. Boards of common pine vary tremendously in quality, though. Look at several boards and pick the ones that have the fewest knots.

Birdhouses Made with Other Materials

Not all birdhouses must be made of wood. Some people make houses out of gourds with holes drilled in them. These are good for wrens and even purple martins, as well as other birds. Many commercial martin houses are made of aluminum painted white. Other commercial houses are made of plastic or ceramics. Each of these materials has certain merits and drawbacks; these are discussed in the chapter "Buying a Birdhouse." For the homemade birdhouse, we recommend wood as the sturdiest and safest material.

This birdhouse placed in a field can attract swallows and house wrens.

Stains, Paints, Finishes

There is no need to paint or stain a birdhouse. The wood can weather naturally and in most cases will last many years. To make the wood last even longer, we recommend the simplest and safest of preservatives: a little pure linseed oil applied to the outside of the birdhouse. If you do this, wait several days until the oil dries before you put the box up for the birds.

Although there is not much that you have to do to finish off your birdhouse, there are many things that you should definitely *not* do. You should not put any preservative, stain, or paint on the inside of the box, on the inside of the entrance hole, or within ¼ inch of the outside of the entrance hole. This ensures that the birds will not suffer any ill effects from contact with these chemicals.

Also, you should not paint the outside of the box with high-gloss paints or finishes or with bright colors, as these may deter the birds from using it. Dark colors may absorb more heat and make the box too hot for the birds. Martin houses are typically painted white, for they are made of thin wood or aluminum and this color helps reflect the light and keeps them cooler.

If you use a paint, finish, or stain other than linseed oil, be sure that it does not contain lead or creosote.

Mounting Your Birdhouse

Before you start constructing your birdhouse, consider how you plan to mount it. You can either mount a house on a vertical surface, such as a tree, fence post, building, or stake, or hang it from a branch or wires.

If you decide to attach the house to a metal garden stake that already has holes, you can just drill holes in the back of the box and attach it with bolts and nuts, provided that one side of the house opens. If you plan to use screws to attach the house, be sure that there is room to reach in with a screwdriver, or design the back panel of the box so that it extends above the top and below the bottom of the house. This way you can drill holes in these extended portions and be able to reach them with a screwdriver without having to maneuver inside the box.

A SUPER EASY BIRDHOUSE

One Size Fits All

This box has been carefully designed so that the dimensions are attractive to a wide variety of birds. We use boxes like this one all over our property and have attracted bluebirds, chickadees, swallows, titmice, wrens, and nuthatches. Starlings are excluded because of the size of the entrance hole. (Note: If you are trying to attract only one specific bird, refer to the special dimensions listed under that species' account in the second half of the book. Those dimensions can be applied to many of the plans shown in the chapter "Advanced Birdhouse Plans.")

Easy to Make

What follows are the plans for one of the easiest birdhouses to make. It can be made with just a handsaw, a hammer, some nails, wood, and a drill. We have purposely adjusted the dimensions so that this design will work given the real widths of the lumber that you commonly buy. The plans — excluding that for the back of the birdhouse, which you will have to draw to scale — are also life-size. You can copy them and use them as a pattern for your wood, or just trace them right off the pages.

Six Simple Steps

1. Draw the life-size patterns on the wood. (Note that back of birdhouse is larger than drawn plan.)
2. Mark where nails go and holes are drilled.
3. Cut out the wood.
4. Drill the holes.
5. Drive nails partially into wood where indicated.
6. Place pieces together and finish nailing.

Buying Wood for the Super Easy Birdhouse

We recommend that you start with common pine. For the super easy birdhouse you will need only two dimensions of pine boards — 1 x 6 inches and 1 x 5 inches. The real dimensions of these boards are ¾ x 5½ inches and ¾ x 4½ inches, and these dimensions will work perfectly with the plan.

To build one birdhouse you will need 28½ inches of the 1 x 6 and 22 inches of the 1 x 5. Most lumber yards will sell boards only by the foot, so you will have to buy extra. You might consider buying enough for two birdhouses at once.

The diagrams below show how the pieces of the birdhouse fit on the lumber.

1 x 5, 22″ long

4″	9″	9″
Bottom	Side	Side

1 x 6, 28½″ long

7½″	9″	12″
Top	Front	Back

The super easy birdhouse as it will look when you are finished.

Plans for the Super Easy Birdhouse

4 inches

4½ inches

This is the BOTTOM of the bird-house. The corners are cut off to allow drainage in case water gets in the box. The gaps also provide some ventilation to the interior of the box.

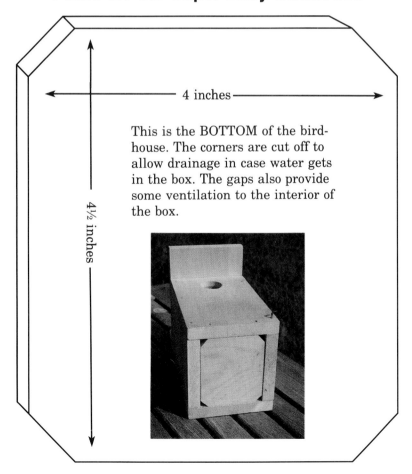

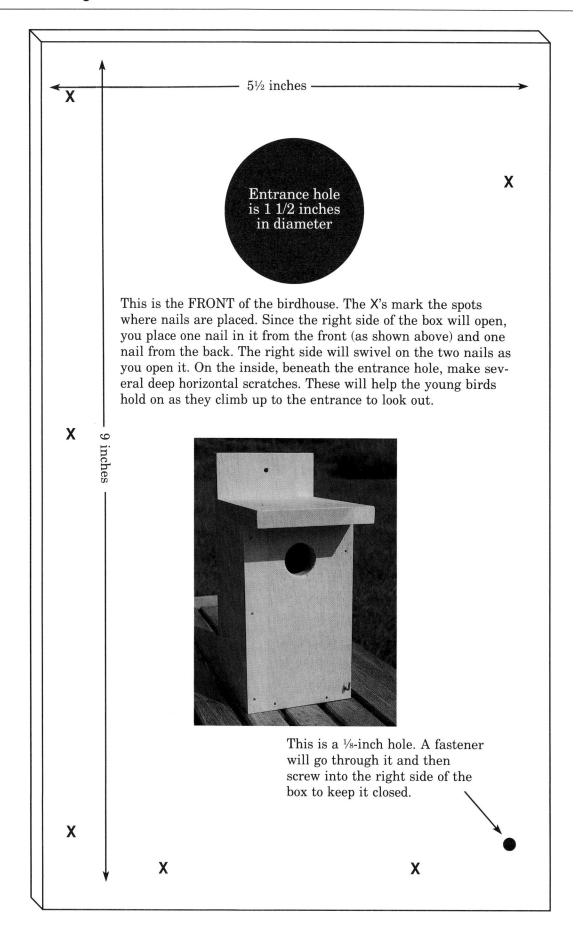

5½ inches

X

Entrance hole
is 1 1/2 inches
in diameter

X

This is the FRONT of the birdhouse. The X's mark the spots
where nails are placed. Since the right side of the box will open,
you place one nail in it from the front (as shown above) and one
nail from the back. The right side will swivel on the two nails as
you open it. On the inside, beneath the entrance hole, make several deep horizontal scratches. These will help the young birds
hold on as they climb up to the entrance to look out.

X

9 inches

This is a ⅛-inch hole. A fastener
will go through it and then
screw into the right side of the
box to keep it closed.

X

X

X

4½ inches

These two holes are each ¼ inch in diameter. They are drilled in both sides of the birdhouse and provide ventilation.

This is the SIDE of the birdhouse. You will need 2 of these, one for the right side and one for the left side.

9 inches

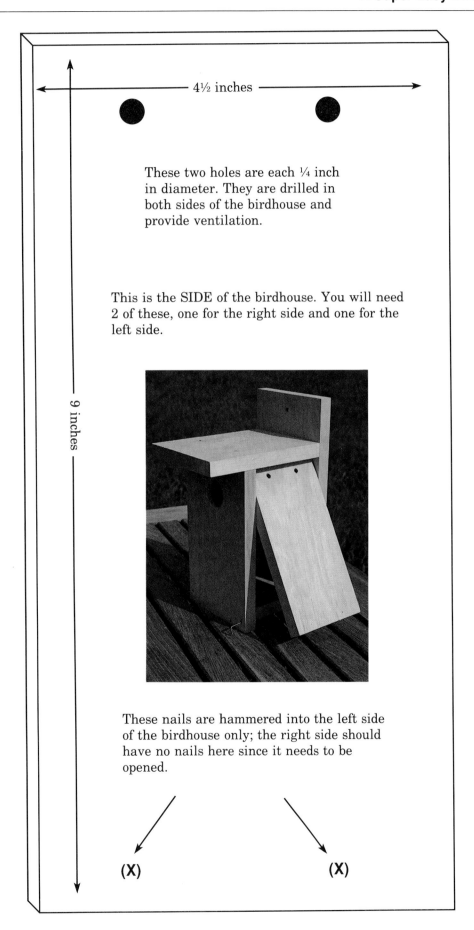

These nails are hammered into the left side of the birdhouse only; the right side should have no nails here since it needs to be opened.

(X)   (X)

5½ inches

X

7½ inches

X

This is the TOP of the birdhouse. It is placed flush against the back and overhangs the front of the box to shelter the entrance hole from rain. The X's mark where the nails will be placed. Note that no nails are hammered into the right side of the box, for this side needs to be free to pivot when it is opened.

X

X

This portion of the top overhangs the front of the box.

5½ inches

X   X

X

This is the BACK of the birdhouse, as you would look at it from the back. The ¼-inch-diameter hole shown above will be used to attach the birdhouse to a tree or pole. The X's mark the spots where nails are placed. To make sure the nails go in the right places, cut this pattern in half along the dotted lines and place each half flush with its end of the cut piece of wood. The bottom of this piece will be flush with the bottom of the box; the top with the hole will stick up above the birdhouse roof.

12 inches
This dimension is not life-size.
It would not fit on this page.

X

X

X   X

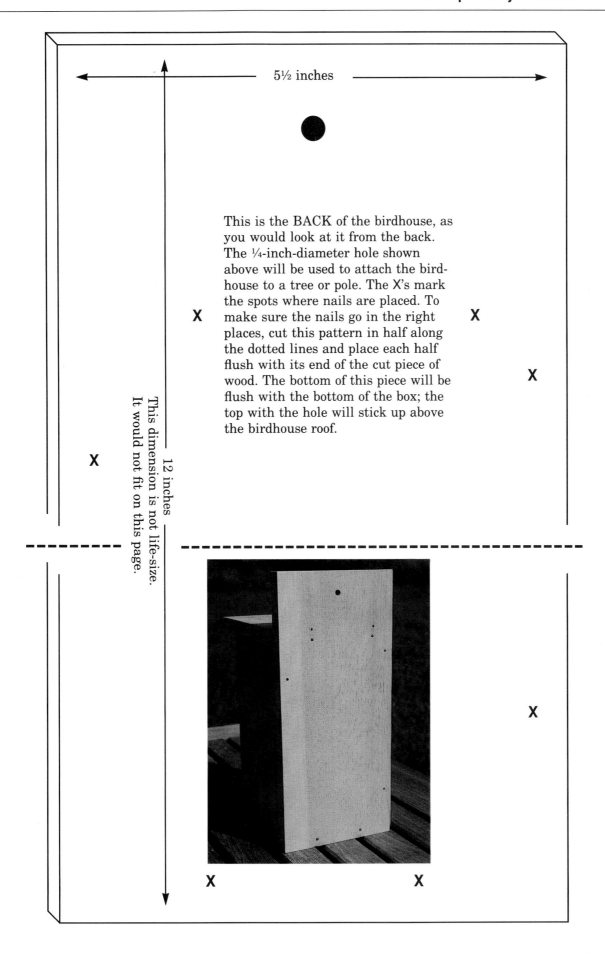

ADVANCED BIRDHOUSE PLANS

The following plans are for the more advanced woodworker with power tools. Some require cuts made on angles other than 90 degrees, and these are best done with a table saw. Others involve curved cuts that are best done with a hand saber saw or a band saw.

The various models shown here will give you some ideas as to how birdhouse design can be varied to suit your own tastes. The dimensions are merely rough guidelines; they will provide you with a sense of the scale of the house. We know that you, as an experienced woodworker, are capable of putting together any of these houses with your own touches.

Detailed dimensions, varied according to the requirements of different birds, are listed under each species account. If you are trying to attract certain species, refer to those dimensions before beginning. Most of these houses can be made for any of our smaller birds. Whether the birds actually prefer one of these models over another has never been tested.

Saltbox Model

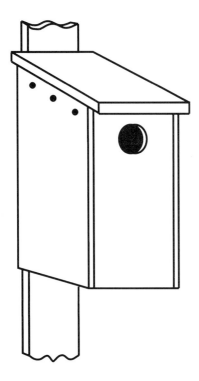

Box dimensions: 6 inches wide, 6 inches deep, 10 inches high

This model is named after the typical New England Colonial house that looked like a salt box with a sloping lid. Its sloping roof is a minor modification of the design for the super easy birdhouse that has the benefit of shedding rainwater off the box. As shown here, you can add a little flair to this box by cutting a design at both ends of the supporting board.

Chalet Model

Box dimensions: 6 inches wide, 6 inches deep, 10 inches high

The chalet model has a pitched roof extending over the sides rather than the front of the house. This is a cute style, one that looks more like human houses. A little ornamentation under the eaves of the house makes it look even more attractive and will not disturb the birds. The model shown here also has sides that slope in at the base of the house. This design feature looks nice but adds some complicated angles in production.

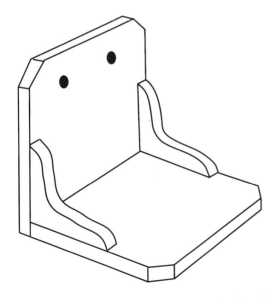

Platform dimensions: 7 inches wide, 7 inches deep

Platform Model

The platform model is just a modified shelf large enough to hold a bird's nest. It can be as simple as a board nailed to a rafter, or more elaborate, as shown. You might even put a roof over it. The platform model shown here does not have a roof since it should be hung under an eave, on a porch, or in a shed where it will be protected. The platform may be more attractive to birds without a roof, since this more closely mimics a little ledge that the birds would find in the wild.

This model can be made to look nicer by cutting a design in the angle supports and taking off the corners as shown.

Martin House Model

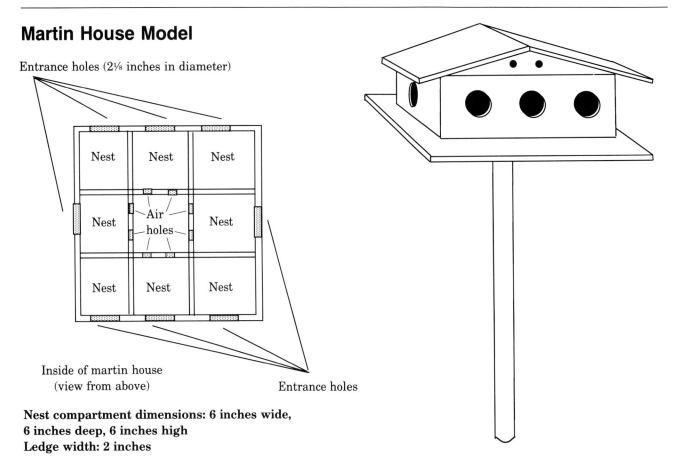

Entrance holes (2⅛ inches in diameter)

Nest | Nest | Nest
Nest | Air holes | Nest
Nest | Nest | Nest

Inside of martin house
(view from above)

Entrance holes

**Nest compartment dimensions: 6 inches wide,
6 inches deep, 6 inches high
Ledge width: 2 inches**

Purple martins will accept colonial living conditions as shown in this martin house. This is a one-story house; more stories can be added. Note that there are nest compartments all around the outside that are roughly 6-inch cubes. In the center is a ventilation chamber that allows air to pass from the nest compartments out through holes just under the roof. The ledge is important, since parents and young birds perch outside the nest at various times in their breeding. The whole struc-

ture needs to be mounted securely on a strong pole. Martin houses are generally painted white, as this reflects the heat and keeps them cooler.

If you build a wooden martin house, place it no higher than 8 feet off the ground so that you can monitor it each week and keep the house sparrows out. In the long run it is better to use one of the modern, commercially available aluminum houses. See the chapter "Martin."

Peterson House

This house is popular among some bluebird enthusiasts. The small floor area is supposed to save the birds time during nest building, for they have to fill less space with nesting material. It is also supposed to leave less room in which blowfly larvae can hide and make cleaning the box easier. The front of the box opens out, pivoting at the base. The entrance hole is slightly oval. See the chapters "Bluebirds" and "Controlling Predators and Competitors."

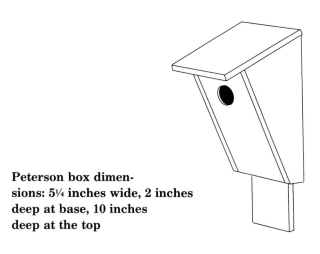

Peterson box dimensions: 5¼ inches wide, 2 inches deep at base, 10 inches deep at the top

Hanging Model

The hanging house model is a good one for many of our smaller birds, such as chickadees, wrens, titmice, and even swallows. Many people call this model a wren house, but there is no reason other small birds will not use it, too. The only potential problem with this model is that the interior space may be too small and the entrance hole too close to the bottom, thus not leaving enough space for the bird's nest. The distance from the base of the hole to the bottom of the box should be at least 5½ inches. This means that the face of the box, which is a square, should be at least 6 inches on a side.

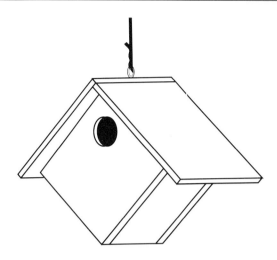

Box dimensions: 6-inch cube

Hexagon dimensions: each of the 6 sides should measure at least 3½ inches on the outside

Hexagonal Model

The hexagonal house has the advantage of more closely simulating a tree with its rounded cavity and rounded exterior. There is no proof, though, that the birds like it better than any other house. It is more difficult to make because of the angles of the hexagon. The roof can be one piece, as shown here, or could be a hexagonal turret. Be sure your interior floor area is roughly the same as that for square boxes designed to attract the same species.

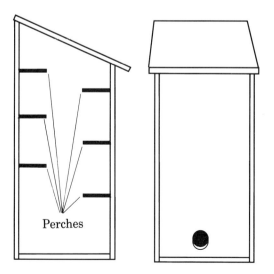

Perches

Roost house dimensions: 10 inches wide, 10 inches deep, 2 feet high; entrance hole 2½ inches in diameter; perches 3 inches long, ⅜ inch in diameter

Roost House Model

The roost box is designed for use in winter, when birds need protection from the extreme cold and often spend the night in tree holes or birdhouses. This design enables several birds to roost in the same spot and, with the opening at the bottom, tends to keep the warmth inside. The perches can be attached either on the sides or on the front and back. When mounting, face box away from prevailing winds.

BLUEBIRDS

Eastern Bluebird — *Sialia sialis*
Mountain Bluebird — *Sialia currucoides*
Western Bluebird — *Sialia mexicana*

Beautiful Bluebirds

Bluebirds are some of America's most beautiful birds. They are a breathtaking sight with plumage truly the color of the sky. Whenever we see one, we are in awe. Bluebirds nest in cavities and birdhouses in open areas with nearby perches from which they can hunt for insects. They are usually quite tolerant of human presence, and are a joy to have nesting on your property.

Success Story

Once a more common bird, bluebirds severely declined in population owing to habitat loss and the introduction of the house sparrow in 1851 and the starling in 1890 — two species that compete heavily for the nesting cavities bluebirds need. Thanks to the efforts of the North American Bluebird Society and the thousands of people who have put up bluebird nesting boxes, bluebird populations are now on the upswing. You can help

---

Quick Guide
Eastern Bluebird

Breeding period: March through July
Territory size: 2–5 acres
Nest materials: Base of fine grasses, pine needles, or weed stalks; inner lining of finer grasses and, rarely, hair or feathers
Eggs: Usually 4 or 5, clear blue or, occasionally, white
Incubation: 12–18 days, average 13–14, by female only
Nestling phase: Usually 17–22 days
Fledgling phase: 2–4 weeks
Broods: 2–3
Migration: Migrates to southern part of range

Bluebird Birdhouse

Dimensions
Entrance-hole diameter:
    Eastern bluebird 1½″
    Mountain bluebird 1⁹⁄₁₆″
    Western bluebird 1⁹⁄₁₆″
Height of hole above floor: 6″–7″
Inside floor dimensions:
    Eastern bluebird 4″ x 4″
    Mountain bluebird 5½″ x 5½″
    Western bluebird 5″ x 5″
Total height of box: 11″–12″

Placement
Habitat: Open areas with low vegetation and a nearby perch
Height: 4′–6′ up on a tree, pole, or fence post

---

make a difference in the success of these beautiful birds by maintaining a bluebird trail. For more information on bluebirds, contact the North American Bluebird Society (see "Resources").

A Bluebird Trail

Although you may want to put up just a single bluebird house, many people put up several at a time in their efforts to attract this lovely bird. Several bluebird houses put up in a given area are often called a "bluebird trail." This term probably derives from the fact that when people put up large numbers of bluebird houses — 50 to several hundred at a time — they are usually placed along roads, fence lines, or trails where they can be easily monitored while driving or hiking.

Birdhouses on a bluebird trail should be placed about 100 yards apart in open, not heavily

Eastern bluebird, male.
Recognized by its blue back, red breast, and white belly.
Female is similar in appearance, but less brightly
colored.

Range Map Key Summer
Range Winter
Range  Year-round
Range

wooded, areas that have short or sparse ground vegetation. Bluebirds like having small trees, shrubs, or other perches within 5 to 100 feet of the box. If you don't have the right habitat for bluebirds on your own property, consider putting a bluebird trail on conservation property in your town or in other appropriate areas with the permission of the landowner.

To maintain a bluebird trail, the boxes must be monitored. See the chapters "Monitoring and Keeping Nest Records" and "Controlling Predators and Competitors." In addition to the standard bluebird house described here, there is another popular design you can use called the Peterson house, named after its inventor, Dick Peterson of Minnesota. See plans on page 46.

Nesting Habits

The nesting habits of the three bluebird species are similar. The male bluebird searches for a territory that includes a good nesting site. He courts a female with sweet warbled notes and by doing a wing-wave — raising and quivering one or both wings. He may feed her tasty morsels as further enticement.

After the female selects a nest box, she does the nest building. Nest building can be done in several days or it can take more than a week.

After an incubation period of about 14 days, the eggs hatch. For the first several days, the female keeps the tiny and practically naked babies

> *Quick Guide*
> **Western Bluebird**
>
> *Breeding period:* March into August
> *Territory size:* 50–400 feet or more between nests
> *Nest materials:* Dried grass, weed stems, pine needles, twigs, sometimes with hair or feathers
> *Eggs:* 3–8, usually 4–6, pale blue or bluish white, rarely white
> *Incubation:* 13–14 days, by female only
> *Nestling phase:* 19–22 days, usually 20–21
> *Fledgling phase:* Possibly 2–3 weeks
> *Broods:* 1–2, rarely 3
> *Migration:* Some birds are resident year-round; others migrate to southern part of their range

Western bluebird, male.
Male has deep blue throat, gray belly, red breast, and sometimes red on deep blue back. Female, grayish on back, blue wings, and light red on breast.

warm by brooding them, while the male brings all of the food. When the young have more feathers and are able to regulate their own body temperature, both parents make food trips.

The babies grow rapidly, more than doubling their weight in a week. Their eyes open on the fourth to seventh day, and they have tail feathers showing by the eighth day. By the fifteenth day, they are completely feathered, and they leave the nest when they are 17 to 22 days old. Do not monitor the box after about the fourteenth day, for the young may leave prematurely.

For 2 to 4 weeks the fledglings are cared for by the parents. Gradually they become proficient flyers and able to feed themselves.

Fledgling bluebirds of all three species have grayish blue backs and brownish spots on white breasts. After a partial molt in early fall, they resemble the adults.

The female may begin a second or, rarely, a third brood in the same or in a different box. Sometimes one or more of the young from a previous brood remain with the parents and actually help raise the nestlings of the following brood by bringing them food.

After breeding, family groups of bluebirds remain near their nesting areas into the autumn, and then drift southward when cold weather sets in. In the winter, they travel in flocks and eat fruits and whatever insects they can find.

Mountain bluebird, male.
Our only all-blue blue-bird, paler on the breast and belly than on the back and head.
Female is grayish-brown with a white belly, except in fall, reddish hue on throat and breast.

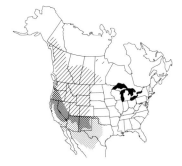

Eastern, Western, and Mountain

The eastern bluebird has a red throat and chest and a white belly. Its range extends over the eastern two-thirds of North America; it is found in suburbs, farmlands, orchards, and open parklands.

The western bluebird has a blue throat, and the brick red color of its chest often extends onto its back. It breeds in western Canada and in the western United States. In some areas, it will nest on the same trails as the mountain bluebird in alternative nest boxes. In the western coastal mountain ranges, western bluebirds may migrate to the valley floors to find good food supplies in winter. Some western bluebirds, however, winter very near where they nested, if the food supply is good.

The mountain bluebird is the "all-blue" blue-bird, lacking the red breast of the eastern and western species. It breeds in open areas in park-

---

Quick Guide
Mountain Bluebird

Breeding period: March into July
Territory size: ¼–1 acre
Nest materials: Strips of bark, dried grass, and other dry plant material
Eggs: 4–7, rarely 8–9, pale blue or sometimes white
Incubation: About 14 days, by female only
Nestling phase: 17–21 days
Fledgling phase: 2–4 weeks
Broods: 1–2
Migration: Migrates to southern part of its range

---

lands, mountains, badlands, and ravines, placing its nest in tree cavities, holes in fence posts or utility poles, and birdhouses.

CHICKADEES

Black-capped Chickadee — *Parus atricapillus*
Carolina Chickadee — *Parus carolinensis*

Chestnut-backed Chickadee — *Parus rufescens*
Mountain Chickadee — *Parus gambeli*

Chickadee Birdhouse

Dimensions
Entrance-hole diameter:
   1⅛"–1½"
Height of hole above floor:
   6"–7"
Inside floor dimensions:
   4" x 4" to 5" x 5"
Total height of box: 9"–12"

Placement
Habitat: Suburban or rural locations with
   a mixture of trees and open areas
Height: 5'–10' up on a tree or post

Carolina chickadee.
Similar to black-capped chickadee, except for its higher version of the "chickadeedee" call. Male and female look alike.

A Cheerful Visitor All Year

A chickadee or two can brighten your day no matter what the season. Watching their constant activity and hearing their tiny calls, one cannot help being intrigued and entertained.

Most of us are familiar with chickadees and their behavior in winter when they are one of the most regular visitors to feeders. But in spring and summer their behavior changes, and the birds go off to breed. If you have birdhouses on your property or suitable trees, you have a good chance of attracting nesting chickadees.

Find One or Make One

In general, chickadees look for tree holes made by woodpeckers or other natural cavities in which to build their nests. But they are also good at making their own cavity, as long as the wood is soft or rotted so that they can excavate it with their short, thin bills.

Trees that typically rot in the center, such as

Quick Guide
Black-capped Chickadee

Breeding period: April to July
Territory size: About 10 acres
Nest materials: Wood chips, moss, hair, feathers, insect cocoons, and other downy fibers
Eggs: 6–8, white with red-brown speckles
Incubation: 12 days, by female only
Nestling phase: 16 days
Fledgling phase: 1–2 weeks
Broods: 1–2
Migration: Generally a year-round resident, but young birds may migrate south

Black-capped chick-adee perched on sumac berries. Recognized by its black cap and chin and white cheeks. Hard to distinguish from the Carolina chickadee except by hearing its lower-pitched "chickadee-dee" call. Male and female look alike.

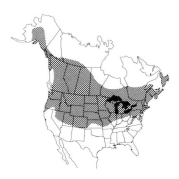

birches, are excellent places for chickadees to excavate. This is one good reason for leaving dead branches or standing dead trees on your property — they provide much-needed nesting spots for hole-nesting birds such as chickadees.

Various Species

There are four species of chickadees that commonly use birdhouses. The Carolina chickadee lives only in the East; the chestnut-backed and mountain chickadees live only in the West, while the black-capped chickadee lives all over.

Mountain Chickadee. Recognized by the white eyebrow going through the black cap. Male and female look alike.

Quick Guide
Carolina Chickadee

Breeding period: April to July
Territory size: About 10 acres
Nest materials: Wood chips, moss, hair, feathers, insect cocoons, down from cinnamon fern
Eggs: 6, white with red-brown speckles
Incubation: 11–12 days, by female only
Nestling phase: 13–17 days
Fledgling phase: 1–2 weeks
Broods: 1–2
Migration: Generally a year-round resident

Quick Guide
Mountain Chickadee

Breeding period: April to July
Territory size: About 10 acres
Nest materials: Wood chips, hair, feathers
Eggs: 7–9, pure white, sometimes with faint spots
Incubation: About 14 days, by female only
Nestling phase: 17–20 days
Fledgling phase: 1–2 weeks
Broods: 1–2
Migration: Generally a year-round resident

The behavior of Carolina and black-capped chickadees is extremely similar; in fact, the two hybridize in various areas where their ranges overlap. The behavior of chestnut-backed and mountain chickadees is less well studied. More observation of their lives needs to occur before we can say with assurance what their behavior is like, although it is probably similar in many ways to that of Carolina and black-capped chickadees. The following accounts are based on studies of Carolina and black-capped chickadees.

The Change from Flock to Pairs

In most species of chickadees, the birds form small flocks in late summer and remain in them until the start of the breeding season the next spring. Just before breeding, the males in these flocks become more aggressive and territorial;

Chestnut-backed Chickadee.
Our only chickadee with a chestnut-brown back. Male and female look alike.

they begin to outline large areas that they defend with chases and song.

Thus, if you have a breeding male in your yard, he will keep out most other chickadees except his mate. Where you had a flock of about 10 birds all winter, you will now have only one pair. The other chickadees have had to move elsewhere to breed.

Courtship and Breeding

Part of chickadee courtship is the male's feeding of the female. He gets an insect or seed and flies to the female, who gives a high, thin call, quivers her wings and takes the food from the male. This is called mate feeding. It continues from the beginning of courtship through the incubation period.

If you go out some morning in early spring, you may be lucky enough to see the pair excavating their nest. The birds do it together, each taking a turn pecking out the wood and then carrying a beakful of sawdust 10 to 20 feet away to drop it. You can get quite close to them as they work, for

they are not easily disturbed in their endeavors.

The female does all the incubating while the male often brings her food. One of the most engaging breeding behaviors is the fledgling phase. For a few weeks then you have the chance to encounter the whole family as they move about the woods together. The young, with their bright, new feathers and high-pitched voices, look adorable as they follow their parents about, begging for food.

Quick Guide
Chestnut-backed Chickadee

Breeding period: March to July
Territory size: About 10 acres
Nest materials: Moss, hair, feathers, and other downy materials
Eggs: 6–7, white with light reddish speckles
Incubation: About 11–12 days, by female only
Nestling phase: About 13–17 days
Fledgling phase: About 1–2 weeks
Broods: 1–2
Migration: Generally a year-round resident

DUCKS

Barrow's Goldeneye — *Bucephala islandica*
Bufflehead — *Bucephala albeola*
Common Goldeneye — *Bucephala clangula*

Common Merganser — *Mergus merganser*
Hooded Merganser — *Lophodytes cucullatus*
Wood Duck — *Aix sponsa*

Cavity-Nesting Ducks

Although most of us never think of ducks as perching or nesting in trees, there are several North American species that regularly do so. These include the wood duck, bufflehead, common and Barrow's goldeneyes, and common and hooded mergansers. The wood duck and hooded merganser are found throughout the East and Northwest; the others breed primarily in the Northwest, Canada, and Alaska.

Efforts to put up birdhouses for ducks in the lower 48 states have centered on the wood duck. But in the Canadian provinces, people also have

Wood duck, fledgling.
This young wood duck is just about to take the plunge from the nest to the ground. Because of its light weight and downy cushioning, it will not get hurt.

**Birdhouse for Ducks
(except the Bufflehead)**

Dimensions
Entrance hole (oval):
 3″ high, 4″ wide for wood duck and hooded merganser; 3½″ high, 4½″ wide for common goldeneye and Barrow's goldeneye; 4″ high, 5″ wide for common merganser
Height of hole above floor:
 16″–18″
Inside floor dimensions:
 10″ x 10″ to 12″ x 12″
Total height of box: 24″–25″

Placement
Habitat: Swamps, shallow lakes, or woods near water, preferably facing water and with no obstructions near entrance hole
Height: At least 4′ up when nest is placed over water and at least 10′ up when placed over land

---

been successful in attracting other species of ducks to birdhouses.

One Small Step for Man, One Giant Step for a Duckling

Imagine yourself to be the young of one of these cavity-nesting ducks. You hatch out of the egg in a dark cavity inside a tree or nest box, and after one day in the nest you hear your mother calling outside the nest. You are drawn to the nest entrance for your first look out and discover that you are anywhere from 3½ to 60 feet above the ground. Mom is telling you to jump, and you can just barely walk, let alone fly.

Wood duck, male.
Our only duck with the long crest that drapes down the back of the head. Male in breeding plumage in unmistakable because of his bright colors. Female is less brightly colored and has a prominent white eye-ring.

This situation is typical for all of the cavity-nesting ducks. On the second day of their lives, the young just jump out of the nest, fall through the air, and, after one bounce off the ground (which never seems to hurt them), are ready to follow their mother to water, if they are not already on it.

Finding a Home

Cavity-nesting ducks are totally incapable of creating or even enlarging a nesting hole in a tree. Therefore, they are entirely dependent on what they can find. They also need to find a large cavity since they are big birds. Large cavities are made only by flickers and pileated woodpeckers; to form naturally from rotting, they have to be in

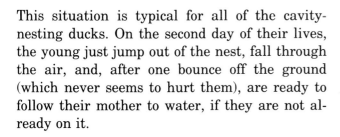

Quick Guide
Wood Duck

Breeding period: April through June
Territory size: Just the nest site
Nest materials: Wood chips, lined with feathers from the female's breast
Eggs: 11–14, white to pale buff
Incubation: 27–30 days, by female only
Nestling phase: 1 day
Fledgling phase: 5 weeks
Broods: 1, occasionally 2 in warm climates
Migration: Northern birds fly to the south

an old tree. A young forest or one without the woodpeckers is not going to provide nesting sites for ducks.

Quick Guide
Bufflehead

Breeding period: May through June
Territory size: Not known
Nest materials: Lined with feathers from the female's breast
Eggs: 8–10, ivory to buff
Incubation: About 29–31 days, by female only
Nestling phase: 1 day
Fledgling phase: About 7–8 weeks
Broods: 1
Migration: Generally migrates south or to coastal areas in winter

Bufflehead Birdhouse

Dimensions
Entrance-hole diameter:
  2½"–3"
Height of hole above floor:
  13"–14"
Inside floor dimensions:
  6" x 6" to 7" x 7"
Total height of box: 17"–19"

Placement
Habitat: Swamps, shallow lakes, or woods near water, preferably facing water and with no obstructions near entrance hole
Height: At least 4' up when nest is placed over water and at least 10' up when placed over land

Feathering Your Nest

None of these ducks seems to bring nesting material into the nest. But they do line cavities with down and feathers from their breasts. Generally there is only a little down when egg laying starts, but later more and more is added. During the incubation period, the female covers over the eggs with the down each time she leaves the nest.

Sometimes you can recognize a tree cavity that is occupied by a nesting duck by seeing bits of down clinging to the nest hole entrance or scattered on the ground below.

A Single-Parent Family

As with many ducks, after the female has started to incubate the eggs, the male of a cavity-nesting pair leaves and has little else to do with raising the young. The ducklings can feed and generally fend for themselves within a day of hatching, so that the female's only duty is to keep them safe from predators. This is better done by the female since she is more camouflaged than the brightly colored male.

After about two weeks, the ducklings are quite independent but still stay with either their

Barrow's goldeneye, male.
Recognized by the white crescent on face in front of eye. Female is similar in appearance to female common goldeneye.

Common goldeneye, female.
Recognized by its brown head, white collar, and golden eye. Its bill is longer than that of the Barrow's goldeneye; otherwise they are similar.

mother or another family of ducks. Little rafts of baby ducks bobbing along with an adult female or two are a common sight in early June.

Special Features of Duck Housing

Several special features are required for duck birdhouses. Young ducklings have to climb to the entrance hole to jump out. To be able to do this, they need a rough surface inside the front of the nest box that they can grab onto. Attaching wire mesh on the inside front or scoring the inside with horizontal saw cuts will suffice. Duck birdhouses should also be filled with wood chips 2 to 4 inches deep to keep the eggs from rolling around and also to provide insulation.

When placing the house, try to angle it slightly

Quick Guide
Barrow's Goldeneye
Common Goldeneye

Breeding period: May into July
Territory size: Just the nest site and feeding area away from nest
Nest materials: Lined with feathers from the female's breast
Eggs: 8–10, olive to light green, slightly darker in the Barrow's goldeneye
Incubation: 30–32 days, by female only
Nestling phase: 1 day
Fledgling phase: About 8 weeks
Broods: 1
Migration: Migrates in winter to large rivers and coastal areas

forward, for this too will make it easier for the ducklings to climb out. Also be sure that the entrance is clear of obstructing branches, for ducks are big birds and need an open path to the nest hole. Once a duck has started to incubate the eggs, do not monitor the nest or the duck may leave.

Protection from Raccoons

Because ducks nest in large cavities near water, they are particularly vulnerable to raccoons, for raccoons feed at water edges, can climb trees, and can reach into the large duck nest holes.

One way to minimize raccoon problems is to place your duck houses out on poles in the water. This is not particularly easy. One recommended way to do it is to go out in the winter on ice that is safe to walk on, poke a hole through the ice, and pound the pole into the pond or lake bottom. Mount the house 4 to 6 feet above the water.

Houses placed on trees at the water's edge should be 10 to 20 feet high. Choose trees close to the water, for the farther the young ducklings have to walk to get there, the more potential danger they face. You can protect the duck houses by putting baffles around the bases of poles or the trunks of trees. For more information on these see the chapter "Controlling Predators and Competitors."

Wood Duck Conservation

Through hunting and habitat destruction, wood ducks became extremely rare in the early 1900s. A conservation effort was begun in the 1930s and 1940s to preserve duck habitats, especially tree cavities, and to put up nesting boxes. This effort was extremely successful, and this is why we are lucky enough to have a healthy population of wood ducks today.

We hope that more efforts will be made to provide houses for all of our cavity-nesting ducks.

Hooded merganser, male.
Recognized by large white patch on head and brown sides of body. Female all dusky.

Bufflehead, male.
Recognized by the large white patch on its greenish head and white sides of body. Female has small white patch on cheek.

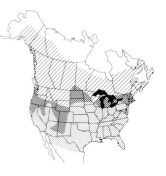

Common merganser, male and female.
Male recognized by very dark head and back and white body. Female is grayish with a reddish crested head.

Quick Guide
Common Merganser

Breeding period: April through June
Territory size: Not known
Nest materials: Lined with feathers from the female's breast
Eggs: 8–11, buff
Incubation: 28–35 days, by female only
Nestling phase: 1 day
Fledgling phase: 10–12 weeks
Broods: 1
Migration: Generally migrates south in winter

Quick Guide
Hooded Merganser

Breeding period: April through June
Territory size: Not known
Nest materials: Lined with feathers from the female's breast
Eggs: 10–12, white
Incubation: 32–33 days, by female only
Nestling phase: 1 day
Fledgling phase: About 10 weeks
Broods: 1
Migration: Generally migrates south in winter

FINCH

House Finch — *Carpodacus mexicanus*

Nests May Be Anywhere

House finches have proved to be very adaptable birds. They have become increasingly accustomed to human habitations, to the point that they are now considered common dooryard birds. They have the added flexibility of being both open-cup and cavity nesters. Because of this their nests can be built in any nook or on any ledge of a building.

They have also been found nesting in tin cans, tree holes, and stovepipes, on the ground, and on branches of cacti, trees, and shrubs. A common nesting spot in the East is baskets of plants hanging on people's porches.

House Finch Birdhouse

Dimensions
Entrance-hole diameter:
  1⅜"–1½"
Height of hole above floor:
  5"–7"
Inside floor dimensions:
  4" x 4" to 5" x 5"
Total height of box: 9"–12"

Placement
Habitat: Near human habitations in urban
  or rural settings
Height: 4'–10' up on a tree, post, or building

Use of Other Birds' Nests

There are many records of house finches appropriating the nests of other birds, either after they are abandoned or even while the other birds are still using them. Species whose nests they commonly use include orioles, phoebes, cliff swallows, and robins.

House finch, male.
This male is at its nest, which is in the cavity of a saguaro cactus.

House finches, male and female, at nest. Male is a sparrow-sized bird with variable amounts of red on head, breast, and rump. Distinguished from similar-looking male finches by heavy brown streaks on sides. Female is brown streaked all over and has no eye stripe as does the similar purple finch.

A House Sparrow Rival

The range of the house finch has been continually expanding over the last seventy-five years in both the East and the West. Some people feel that this finch is competing with house sparrows for nesting sites in urban areas. The range expansion and adaptability to a variety of nest sites are not necessarily good for other cavity nesters. It means that there will be more competition for nest holes — an already scarce commodity. Only in future years and through population studies will we know the effect of house finch expansion.

Quick Guide
House Finch

Breeding period: March into July
Territory size: Just the immediate area
around the nest site
Nest materials: Twigs, leaves, rootlets,
grasses, and other debris
Eggs: 4–5, white to pale buff
Incubation: 12–14 days, by female only
Nestling phase: 11–19 days
Fledgling phase: 5 weeks
Broods: 1–3
Migration: Generally a year-round resident

Courtship and Song

The male and, occasionally, the female house finches sing a lovely, rich, warbling song. The song is only a few seconds long, but the bird tends to string several songs together in a row, making them sound almost continuous. House finch song occurs most often as part of courtship in late winter and spring, just before breeding, but bits of song can be heard in summer, fall, and even in winter on a warm day.

Another courtship activity of the pair is mate feeding. The male gets food and brings it to the female, who quivers her wings as she takes it. Many people see this behavior at their feeders in late winter and spring. This continues through the incubation phase.

House and Purple Finches

People often confuse house finches with purple finches. Our recommendation is to ignore the oft-cited amount of red on the heads of the males, for this varies among individuals, and look for brown streaks along the sides of the belly. The male purple finch has no brown streaking on the sides; the male house finch has heavy brown streaks along its sides.

FLYCATCHERS

Ash-throated Flycatcher — *Myiarchus cinerascens*
Great Crested Flycatcher — *Myiarchus crinitus*

Ash-throated flycatcher.
The only western flycatcher with an olive head and back and a bright rusty tail. Male and female look alike.

Flycatcher Birdhouse

Dimensions
Entrance-hole diameter:
  1½"–2½"
Height of hole above floor:
  6"–7"
Inside floor dimensions:
  5" x 5" to 6" x 6"
Total height of box: 9"–12"

Placement
Habitat: In old orchards or at the edge of woods
Height: 6'–20' up on a tree or post

Snake Skins

The great crested flycatcher has long been famous for its use of shed snake skins as a nesting material. Snake skins are found in about one-half to two-thirds of the nests. In general, only small portions of the skins are incorporated into the nest lining, but occasionally a larger portion, such as that shown in the photograph on the facing page, is used.

Quick Guide
Ash-throated Flycatcher

Breeding period: March into July
Territory size: Not known
Nest materials: Hair, fur, fine grasses, occasionally shed reptile skins
Eggs: 4–5, creamy white with elongated blotches of brown
Incubation: About 15 days, by female only
Nestling phase: 14–16 days
Fledgling phase: About 1 week
Broods: 1
Migration: Migrates to Mexico

Speculation as to why the bird uses snake skins has suggested that the skins may scare off predators that are afraid of snakes. It is more likely that snake skins are simply a good material for the nest, for great crested flycatchers will also use cellophane and other materials with a texture similar to that of snake skins. Ash-throated flycatchers have been known also to use snake or lizard skins in their nests, but much less frequently than the great crested flycatcher.

Secondary Cavity Nesters

These flycatchers are secondary cavity nesters, which means that they cannot make their own nest holes. They generally use rotted-out portions of tree trunks or snags. They also may use abandoned woodpecker holes. In some instances they have taken over nest holes while woodpeckers were in the process of excavating them.

Both of these flycatchers readily use bird-houses. They are fairly large birds and need an entrance hole at least 1½ inches in diameter. As forests were cleared in the East by early settlers, great crested flycatchers adapted to using any cavity they could find, which later included gutters and mailboxes.

Elusive But Noisy

Both of these flycatchers are heard more often than they are seen. The great crested flycatcher usually stays up in the treetops, since it feeds on

Great crested flycatcher.
Recognized by its large size, olive back and head, yellow belly, and bright rusty tail. Male and female look alike.

insects in the canopy. Its most familiar calls are a very loud ascending "wheeep" and a loud, short, gargling note. This species may give a more extended and somewhat musical sound in the pre-dawn hours.

Both these birds are called flycatchers because of their feeding behavior. They tend to sit on exposed perches looking for insects. When they spot one, they fly out and catch it in midair or on the ground. They are very adept at this, being able even to pick off dragonflies, which are among the best flyers among insects.

Quick Guide
Great Crested Flycatcher

Breeding period: March into July
Territory size: Not known
Nest materials: Grass, pine needles, fur, feathers, bits of bark, cloth, or paper, and quite often bits of shed snake skins
Eggs: 5–6, creamy white with elongated blotches of brown
Incubation: 12–15 days, by female only
Nestling phase: 14–21 days
Fledgling phase: About 1 week
Broods: 1
Migration: Migrates to Central America

KESTREL

American Kestrel — *Falco sparverius*

Success with Birdhouses

Many people have been successful in attracting American kestrels to birdhouses. The kestrel cannot excavate its own hole and is to a great degree dependent on finding the larger nest holes of flickers or pileated woodpeckers in which to nest.

These are often in short supply and this, rather than lack of food, may be the main controlling factor in kestrel populations. Birdhouses placed

American kestrel, fledgling.
The downy tufts on the head of this bird show that it is still a juvenile and has not acquired all of its adult feathers.

Kestrel Birdhouse

Dimensions
Entrance-hole diameter: 3"
Height of hole above floor:
  10"–12"
Inside floor dimensions:
  8" x 8" to 9" x 9"
Total height of box: 14"–16"

Placement
Habitat: Open fields or the edge of woods
Height: 15'–30' up on a tree or post

in open areas, such as along highways, have been readily used by kestrels, and as more boxes are put up, the population and density increase. Some people recommend that 2 to 3 inches of wood chips be placed in the bottom of the box; others have found that the kestrels just push this away and lay their eggs on the bare wood.

Eats Voles and Insects

The American kestrel used to be called the sparrow hawk, but this was definitely a misnomer since the bird feeds almost exclusively on larger insects, such as grasshoppers and crickets, and meadow voles — small mouselike animals living primarily in open grassy areas.

The kestrel can catch and eat small birds but only occasionally does so. Still, because of this ability, you may not want to place a kestrel birdhouse near other birdhouses or in your yard. It is better to put it in large open fields or orchards, where you can profit from the bird's eating of voles and insects that can damage certain crops.

American kestrel, female, bringing a cricket to feed her young.
The kestrel can be identified by the two black "whiskers" on the side of the face, its small size, and its rusty back. The female, as shown here, has brown wings, while the male has steel-blue wings.

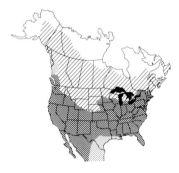

Breeding Habits

One of the most conspicuous behaviors seen around the nest site is the bringing of food by the male to the female. Once the two have paired and chosen a nest site, the female tends to remain near the nest and has most of her food brought to her. This continues through egg laying and incubation, and into the nestling phase — a period of up to 11 weeks.

After the young leave the nest, they will perch together in trees, making short flights and waiting for either parent to bring them food. They flutter their wings and give a whining call when the adults approach. In the first days after leaving the nest, they may return to it at night.

Quick Guide
American Kestrel

Breeding period: April through June
Territory size: Average 250 acres, but variable
Nest materials: No lining or additional materials are added to natural cavities
Eggs: 4–5, whitish with small brown dots
Incubation: 30 days, by female only
Nestling phase: About 30 days
Fledgling phase: 2 weeks
Broods: 1
Migration: Migrates south from northern areas

MARTIN

Purple Martin — *Progne subis*

Most Wanted Bird

America's Most Wanted Bird is the title of a book written in 1966 by J. L. Wade. This book, along with the author's efforts in the 1960s, made the putting up of martin houses a national pastime. Since that time, thousands of martin houses have been placed in parks and backyards. These have undoubtedly increased the populations of this much-loved bird.

The Modern Martin House

For hundreds of years, people have been putting up houses to attract purple martins. They have usually been groups of gourds with entrance holes or large birdhouses with many compartments. In the eastern half of the United States purple martins seem to like these colonial nesting situations. In the West, many purple martins

Purple martins in a colony-type birdhouse.
Martins are our largest swallow, and the male is our only swallow that is all dark-colored. The female is dark above and light below.

Purple Martin Birdhouse
Dimensions
Entrance hole diameter: 2″–2½″, ideally 2⅛″
Height of hole above floor: 1″
Inside floor dimensions: 6″ x 6″
Total height of box: 6″
Placement
Habitat: Open areas near human habitations, preferably with water nearby
Height: 8′–20′ up on a post

nest singly in old woodpecker holes and other crevices. From this evidence, it would seem that the eastern and western populations of purple martins have different nesting behaviors.

The ideal martin house should have the following components and characteristics: nest compartments that measure 6 inches wide, deep, and high; 2⅛-inch-diameter entrance holes; white nest-compartment interiors to discourage starlings; good ventilation and drainage; plugs for the entrance holes in winter to keep out starlings and house sparrows; nest compartments that open easily so that any sparrow nests can be cleaned out; and a means of easily lowering and raising the whole house for weekly inspection.

This last component is essential, for it prevents a martin house from becoming just another place for house sparrows to breed. Sparrow nests must be cleaned out of martin houses each week. This can be quite a chore unless the house is light. This is why most good martin houses are made of aluminum and placed on steel poles that have a winch or pulley attached for easy raising and lowering.

Purple martins nesting in gourds that are painted white and hung from poles. These are extremely popular in the Southeast, and martins seem to prefer them to the colony-type house. The gourds seem to moderate the effects of cooler and hotter weather.

Classic Study of Martin Birdhouses

In 1974, the results of a long-term study of martin birdhouses by J. A. Jackson and J. Tate, Jr., were published. The associated survey was completed by 1,067 people in 32 states, answering various questions about the structure, care, and placement of martin birdhouses. It was found that the height of martin houses had little effect on occupancy; martin houses less than 30 yards from buildings had more martins than those farther away; the fewest house sparrows were in colonies made out of gourds (as shown above); there was no significant difference in the occupancy rates of aluminum versus wooden houses; there was no significant preference shown for a particular exterior color; martins may prefer nest sites that are not cleaned out from the previous year; houses in urban and rural sites had more birds than those in suburban areas; starlings are not a

threat to martin colonies since they are territorial, and one nesting pair keeps others away; and finally, house sparrows can be a disturbance to martins, since they nest colonially and may take over a single colony-type martin birdhouse.

Quick Guide
Purple Martin

Breeding period: May into August
Territory size: Immediate area of nest hole
Nest materials: Grass stems, twigs, paper, mud, and green leaves
Eggs: 5–6, pure white
Incubation: 15–16 days, by female only
Nestling phase: 27–35 days
Fledgling phase: About 1 week
Broods: 1
Migration: Migrates to South America

NUTHATCHES

Red-breasted Nuthatch — *Sitta canadensis*
White-breasted Nuthatch — *Sitta carolinensis*

Nature's Wind-up Toy

When we watch nuthatches climb up and down tree trunks in their stop-and-go manner, we are always reminded of an engaging little wind-up toy. They are charming and almost comical birds to have at your feeders, and although they do not take to birdhouses as readily as many other birds, they are definitely worth trying to attract.

Which Species?

There are four species of nuthatches in North America — the white-breasted, red-breasted, pygmy, and brown-headed. The white-breasted nuthatch almost always looks for a cavity already made either by another bird or through natural causes. The other three species are more likely to excavate their own holes in soft, partially rotted wood.

Nuthatch Birdhouse

Dimensions
Entrance-hole diameter:
   $1\frac{1}{8}''-1\frac{1}{2}''$
Height of hole above floor: 6″–7″
Inside floor dimensions:
   4″ x 4″ to 5″ x 5″
Total height of box: 9″–12″

Placement
Habitat: Suburban or rural woods, or locations with a mixture of trees and open space
Height: 5′–10′ up on a tree or post

Because of this, the white-breasted nuthatch is the most likely of the four to be attracted to a birdhouse.

Red-breasted nuthatch, male. Recognized by its dark cap, white eyebrow, and black line through the eye. Male has black cap and reddish breast; female has silver cap and buff breast.

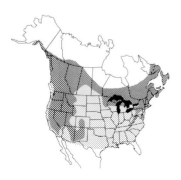

Of the other three, the red-breasted nuthatch has been recorded as the most frequent user of birdhouses. The brown-headed and pygmy nuthatches rarely use birdhouses.

Beetle Sweeping

Imagine sweeping your front porch by holding a beetle in your mouth and rubbing it against the floor. This is what nuthatches do around the entrances to their nest holes. It is believed that by doing this they leave a residue of a chemical secreted defensively by the beetle, which may deter certain nest predators from entering the hole.

Roost Hole

Nuthatches may use your birdhouses all winter as well, for then they commonly have holes in which they roost each night. In the case of white-breasted nuthatches, which stay in the same area all year, male and female may have separate roost holes. The pygmy nuthatches, by contrast, are reported as forming communal roosts of 4 to 15 birds in a single nest cavity.

Storing Food

Not only do nuthatches store food in bark crevices in winter for later use, they do the same around the nest box when breeding. This is subsequently retrieved and fed to the female while she is incubating or to the developing nestlings.

White-breasted nuthatch, male. Recognized by its dark cap and white cheek and throat. Nuthatches are one of our few birds that climb down trees head-first. Male has black cap; female has silver cap.

Quick Guide
White-breasted Nuthatch

Breeding period: March through June
Territory size: 25–45 acres
Nest materials: Bark, grasses, rootlets, fur
Eggs: 5–10, white with small brown speckles
Incubation: 12 days, by female only
Nestling phase: About 14 days
Fledgling phase: About 2 weeks
Broods: 1
Migration: Generally a year-round resident

Quick Guide
Red-breasted Nuthatch

Breeding period: May through July
Territory size: 20–30 acres
Nest materials: Bark shreds, roots, grasses
Eggs: 5–6, white with small brown speckles
Incubation: 12 days, by female only
Nestling phase: 14–21 days
Fledgling phase: 1–2 weeks
Broods: 1, possibly 2
Migration: Migrates south in the winter when cone production is poor in the North

OWLS

Barred Owl — *Strix varia*
Common Barn Owl — *Tyto alba*
Eastern Screech Owl — *Otus asio*

Northern Saw-whet Owl — *Aegolius acadicus*
Western Screech Owl — *Otus kennicottii*

Owl Nesting Habits

None of our North American owls builds nests. The 5 species mentioned here all nest in cavities and readily take to birdhouses. There are 8 other North American species of owls that nest in cavities, but they do not normally use birdhouses.

Northern saw-whet owl peering out from its nest.
A small owl with dark bill, no ear tufts, and reddish-brown facial disk. Male and female look alike.

Owl Birdhouse
Northern Saw-whet Owl
Eastern Screech Owl
Western Screech Owl

Dimensions
Entrance-hole diameter:
  2½"–4"
Height of hole above floor:
  10"–12"
Inside floor dimensions:
  6" x 6" to 8" x 8"
Total height of box: 15"–18"

Placement
Habitat: Screech owls — in or at the edge of woods, in urban or rural areas; Saw-whet owls — in deep woods, preferably near swamps
Height: 5'–20' up on a tree, post, or building

For a list of all cavity-nesting owls, see "Who Nests Where," pages 8–9.

Our other owls, which do not live in cavities, also do not build nests. Two of these, the snowy owl and short-eared owl, nest on the ground. One species, the burrowing owl, nests in old mammal burrows. And the other three, the great gray, great horned, and long-eared owls, use the abandoned open-cup nests of other birds, such as those of crows and hawks, or the nests of squirrels.

Who Gives a Hoot?

Although it is commonly believed that all owls hoot, the fact is that only a few do; all the others make a variety of screeches, caterwauls, and whistles. Of the cavity-nesting owls mentioned here, only the barred owl hoots. Its familiar call is four hoots in a phrase that sounds like "Who

Barred owl and young at nest.

Recognized by its large size, all-dark eyes, barring on its upper breast, and streaks on its lower breast. Male and female look alike.

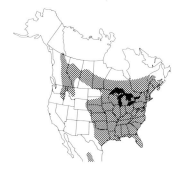

cooks for you?" The barred owl also gives many other calls that range from something like maniacal laughter to the howls of monkeys.

The saw-whet owl is named for its call. To "whet" a saw you grip it in a vise and run a small file over it. The resulting sound is similar to the saw-whet owl's repeated short whistles.

The screech owl, eastern and western, does not really screech. Rather, its two main vocalizations are a descending quavering whistle and a continuous series of notes on one pitch.

The barn owl makes some of the most unusual of all bird sounds. One of its calls resembles the screech of metal scraping against metal. Another is similar to the sound of a tremendous rush of steam coming out of an engine. Hearing these calls in the dead of night can be either terribly frightening or terribly exciting, depending on your perspective.

Quick Guide
Northern Saw-whet Owl

Breeding period: March into July
Territory size: Not known
Nest materials: None
Eggs: 5–6, pure white
Incubation: 26–28 days, mostly by female
Nestling phase: 28–33 days
Fledgling phase: Not known
Broods: 1, occasionally 2
Migration: Some migrate from northern areas

Quick Guide
Barred Owl

Breeding period: March into August
Territory size: About 1 square mile
Nest materials: None
Eggs: 2–3, white
Incubation: 28–33 days, mostly by female
Nestling phase: 4–7 weeks or longer
Fledgling phase: Several weeks
Broods: 1
Migration: Generally a year-round resident

Eastern screech owl and young at nest.
Adult western and eastern screech owls look similar — small owls with yellow eyes and prominent ear tufts. Male and female look alike.

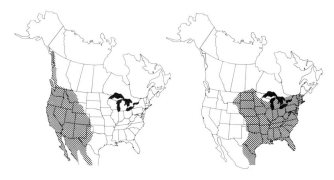

Quick Guide
Eastern Screech Owl
Western Screech Owl

Breeding period: March into July
Territory size: Just the area around the nest site
Nest materials: None
Eggs: 4–6, white
Incubation: 27–30 days, by female only
Nestling phase: About 4 weeks
Fledgling phase: 6–8 weeks
Broods: 1
Migration: Generally a year-round resident

Barn Owl Birdhouse

Dimensions
Entrance-hole diameter: 6″–8″
Height of hole above floor: 4″
Inside floor dimensions:
  16″ wide, 22″ deep
Total height of box: 16″

Placement
Habitat: Open farmland
Height: 10′–20′ up on a tree, a barn, or a shed

Barred Owl Birdhouse

Dimensions
Entrance-hole diameter: 6″–8″
Height of hole above floor:
  14″–18″
Inside floor dimensions:
  13″ x 13″ to 14″ x 14″
Total height of box: 22″–28″

Placement
Habitat: Woods or swamps in suburban or rural areas
Height: 10′–20′ up on a tree

Daily Schedule

The daytime program for owls is generally to sleep and stay still; some owls, however, are more "day owls" than "night owls." One of these is the barred owl, which you can hear hooting in the middle of a summer day. Barred owls do most of their hunting at night, as do the other owls, but they also make short flights around the nesting area during the day.

Activity for most owls starts when it begins to get dark. The birds stir, stretch, and often regurgitate pellets containing the indigestible fur and bones of animals they caught and ate the previous night. Then they usually go off to hunt, returning before dawn. If they are having trouble finding enough food at night, their hunting may continue into the dawn hours.

Quick Guide
Barn Owl

Breeding period: March into July
Territory size: Just the area around the nest site
Nest materials: Lined with leaves, rootlets, grasses, and other debris
Eggs: 4–5, white to pale buff
Incubation: 30–34 days, by male and female
Nestling phase: 52–56 days
Fledgling phase: 2–3 weeks
Broods: 1–2
Migration: Migrates slightly south from northern areas

Owl Diets

The two largest owls mentioned here, the barn and barred owls, eat meadow voles and other rodents almost exclusively. The three smaller owls have a more varied diet. Screech owls may feed on night-flying insects. When nesting in the city, they may frequent the areas under streetlights to which moths and other insects are attracted.

These smaller owls can also eat other small birds that may be roosting on branches at night. Because of this you may not want owl birdhouses right near those of your other birds.

Tree-Climbing Owls

Both barred and screech owls have the ability as nestlings and young fledglings to climb trees. This is a useful trait because they often leave the nest hole before they can fly. If they have been nesting in a tree hole, to get to a perch they just work their way up the trunk, basically crawling, using their beaks, talons, and wings.

This also means that if for some reason they fall out of a tree before they can fly, they will be able to get back up to the safety of the treetop. Barred owl fledglings can climb as high as 50 feet up a tree in 20 minutes.

Barn Owl.
Easily recognized by its white, heart-shaped face. Male and female look alike.

Competing for Nest Holes

Screech and saw-whet owls are so small that they may compete for some of the natural cavities and birdhouses that can be used by other birds. For example, screech owls and saw-whet owls commonly use old flicker nest holes, which are about 2½ inches in diameter. Other birds that might like to use these holes include the great crested and ash-throated flycatchers, American kestrel, purple martin, and red-bellied and red-headed woodpeckers. In fact, screech owls have been reported to nest in purple martin birdhouses.

SPARROW

House Sparrow — *Passer domesticus*

The "English" Sparrow

The house sparrow is sometimes referred to as the "English" sparrow because in the 1850s it was imported to North America from England. Its population peaked around 1900, but when the automobile arrived on the scene, the number of sparrows declined significantly. The reason for the decline was that the sparrows fed on the discarded bits of oats fed to horses. With cars on the ascendance and horses on the wane, there were fewer oat bits and consequently fewer sparrows. Still, the little bird is a ubiquitous denizen of cities and suburbs.

House sparrows, like starlings, compete with native cavity-nesting species of birds for nest holes. Because of this they should be discouraged from nesting in your birdhouses. For details about how to do this, see "Controlling Predators and Competitors," page 26.

City Nesters

The house sparrow is one of the few cavity nesters that are really at home in the city. These birds will nest in any cavity that they can find, including air conditioners, street lamps, store awnings, and neon signs. In these situations the sparrow is not competing with any of our native birds and so doesn't need to be disturbed.

One of the most common sights around these nests is the male sitting on a nearby perch repeatedly calling "chirup, chireep, chirup." This is called the nest-site call and serves to attract a female. If a female comes near, the male calls louder and his wings begin to quiver. If the female stays, the male starts to go in and out of the nest cavity, as if to show her where it is. If she, in turn, goes into the nest cavity, there is a good chance that the two are now paired.

House sparrow, male, nesting in a saguaro cactus.
A small, brown bird with an unstreaked breast and black around the chin and eye. Female is all buff-colored and lacks the black on its face.

Quick Guide
House Sparrow

Breeding period: March into August
Territory size: Area right around the nest
Nest materials: Grasses, leaves, twigs, cloth, feathers
Eggs: 4–6, whitish, marked with irregular brown dots
Incubation: 12 days, by female only
Nestling phase: 15–17 days
Fledgling phase: About a week
Broods: 2–3
Migration: Year-round resident

STARLING

European Starling — *Sturnus vulgaris*

A Strong Competitor

In 1890, the European starling was introduced into New York City, and since that time its population and range have exploded. It is now common all across the United States and southern Canada. This presents a problem, for the starling lives in cavities and competes with all of our other native cavity-nesting species. It also happens to be very aggressive and can oust these other birds from their homes, even those a little larger than itself.

Because of this, it is not advisable to encourage starlings to nest in your birdhouses. For how to discourage them, see "Controlling Predators and Competitors," page 26.

Nest Site Displays

There are, nevertheless, many times when you cannot control where starlings nest. This is the case in cities, where they nest in the crevices of buildings, or in the country, where they nest in tree holes too high to reach. In these situations you might as well sit back and at least enjoy some of the starlings' behavior.

Male starlings may start to defend nesting sites as early as fall. They do this by perching near the site and giving a crowing call that sounds like a jumble of whistled and screeched sounds. If another male starling lands on the branch, the owner performs the comical action of "sidling": it keeps stepping sideways toward the intruder, forcing it farther and farther out on the branch, until it finally has to fly away or fall off. Male starlings try to defend nest sites in fall, hoping to retain ownership into the breeding season the next spring. This early defense behavior probably developed as a result of the extreme competition for cavities.

European starling, winter plumage.
In winter it is a black bird heavily speckled with white, with a dark bill. In summer it is a black bird with a yellow bill. Male and female look similar.

Quick Guide
European Starling

Breeding period: March into July
Territory size: The area right around the nest
Nest materials: Dead leaves, moss, lichens, bark, grasses, tree flowers
Eggs: 4–5, pale bluish or greenish white
Incubation: 12 days, by male and female
Nestling phase: 23 days
Fledgling phase: 4–8 days
Broods: 1–2
Migration: Generally a year-round resident

SWALLOWS

Tree Swallow — *Tachycineta bicolor*
Violet-green Swallow — *Tachycineta thalassina*

Built-in Bug Catchers

Swallows are wonderful to have nesting on your property, for they are constantly swooping about, catching insects in their wide mouths. Of course, whether they catch insects that are actually bothering us, such as mosquitoes, is another matter. Chances are they do not, since the mosquitoes are more active after the swallows have retired for the night.

Violet-green swallow. Distinguished from the tree swallow by the white on its cheek, which extends above the eye. Male darker and more iridescent green than female.

> **Swallow Birdhouse**
>
> *Dimensions*
> *Entrance-hole diameter:*
>   1¼″–1½″
> *Height of hole above floor:* 6″–7″
> *Inside floor dimensions:*
>   4″ x 4″ to 5″ x 5″
> *Total height of box:* 9″–12″
>
> *Placement*
> *Habitat:* Open fields or open woods near
>   water
> *Height:* 4′–10′ up on a tree or post

Cooperative Nesters

These two swallows are very easy to attract. Simply place boxes out in the open in rural or suburban areas. The violet-green swallow is slightly more of a suburban bird than the tree swallow, but both are very comfortable near humans.

The tree swallow is slightly larger than the violet-green swallow and will prefer the larger entrance-hole dimension of 1½ inches. The violet-green swallow will also be happy with this size.

Your Own Swallow Colony

Once swallows successfully nest on your property, chances are that the adults and their young will return the next year to breed. If you put up additional boxes each year, you will find your swallow colony growing. We have had as many as 13 pairs nesting on our 2-acre field. It is wonderful to walk out among them and have them all flying about overhead. The only limits to the size of your colony may be the number of boxes you are willing to put up and the abundance of insects in the area.

Put Out Feathers for Fun

Both of these swallows habitually line their nests with feathers. Sometimes they have to go quite a distance to find them. One of our neighbors keeps chickens, so the nests in our colony usually have white chicken feathers, although we also have found pheasant and grouse feathers in our swallows' nests.

If you can get some chicken feathers, take them out to where the swallows are nesting. Throw a few up in the air, and you may find that the birds are stimulated to dive after them. If not, just leave them on the ground or in a string bag for the birds to use.

Sometimes you will see a swallow pick up a feather, carry it high into the air, drop it, and then swoop around and catch it again. At other times you may see one bird chasing another that is carrying a feather in its bill.

Vulnerable to Bad Weather

When the weather gets rainy or cold for extended periods, swallows have trouble collecting enough insects to feed themselves or to support their growing nestlings. Then the adults may leave the colony for a day or two to find insects elsewhere. Their departure can result in the death of the young. This is always a sad event, but you will be glad to know that the adults will return and start a second nesting. This nesting is usually successful, since it is well past the time of extended cold weather.

Tree swallow.
Recognized by its dark blue-green on top and its pure white below. Female and male are very similar.

Quick Guide
Violet-green Swallow

Breeding period: April through July
Territory size: A few feet around the nest
Nest materials: Straw, grasses, string, hair, feathers for lining
Eggs: 4–6, pure white
Incubation: 13–14 days, by female only
Nestling phase: About 21 days
Fledgling phase: 2–3 days
Broods: 1–2
Migration: Migrates to Central America

Quick Guide
Tree Swallow

Breeding period: April through July
Territory size: A few feet around the nest
Nest materials: Grasses, then lined with feathers
Eggs: 5–6, pure white
Incubation: 14–15 days, by female only
Nestling phase: About 21 days
Fledgling phase: 2–3 days
Broods: 1
Migration: Migrates to southern United States and Central America

TITMICE

Plain Titmouse — *Parus inornatus*
Tufted Titmouse — *Parus bicolor*

One of the Best

Titmice are among the easiest birds to attract. If you live in a suburban or rural area and have bird feeders and birdhouses on your property, you have a good chance of having titmice nest in your yard. They are very comfortable around human habitations and are generally not afraid of people.

Plain titmouse.
A small, all-gray bird with a crest. Male and female look alike.

Titmouse Birdhouse

Dimensions
Entrance-hole diameter:
  1⅜″–1½″
Height of hole above floor: 6″–7″
Inside floor dimensions:
  4″ x 4″ to 5″ x 5″
Total height of box: 9″–12″

Placement
Habitat: Suburban or rural locations with a mixture of trees and open areas
Height: 5′–10′ up on a tree or post

In addition, they are the real busybodies among the backyard birds, curious about everything that goes on in the area and seeming to scold forever, even long after the slightest disturbance, imagined or otherwise, has left off or gone away.

Tufted titmice have always been common in the South and in recent years have expanded their range far into the North. Some of this expansion may be a result of the tremendous popularity of bird feeding. In the West, the plain titmouse is the tufted titmouse's counterpart. The behavior of the two species is quite similar, and the behavioral accounts that follow apply equally well to both.

Enjoying Titmouse Behavior

Titmouse breeding behavior starts in late winter with males giving their clear, down-slurred whistles: "Peer, peer, peer . . . peer, peer, peer." At this time males begin to defend small territories of a few acres, and the winter flocks that have been coming to your feeders break up.

Fairly soon you will see just mated pairs flying about together. Part of their courtship is mate

Tufted titmouse.
A small, gray bird with a crest and a black patch just above the bill. Male and female look alike.

feeding, when the male gets food and presents it to the female, beak to beak. She usually gives a high-pitched call and quivers her wings when receiving it.

Starting around late March, you may see the birds inspecting nest boxes. If you leave a string bag full of hair or fur, such as that combed from a dog or cat, hanging near your bird feeders, the titmice will find it irresistible. They will carry large wads of these materials back to their nest. This is a good way to locate the nest — just follow the birds. The female does all the building, but the male may follow her about as she does so.

When the female is incubating the eggs, you may see the male approach with food and give a soft "peer, peer, peer" song. The female will come out of the nest at this signal, take the food from the male, and then continue incubating.

Later, when the young have hatched and fledged, you may see the whole family group flying about together. The young are very noisy at this time and give a variety of calls.

Quick Guide
Plain Titmouse

Breeding period: March through July
Territory size: 2–5 acres
Nest materials: Mosses, hair, grasses, feathers
Eggs: 6–8, white, sometimes with small brown dots
Incubation: 14–16 days, by female only
Nestling phase: 16–21 days
Fledgling phase: 3 or more weeks
Broods: 1, possibly 2
Migration: Year-round resident

Quick Guide
Tufted Titmouse

Breeding period: March through June
Territory size: 2–5 acres
Nest materials: Mosses, hair, grasses, leaves, cotton, wool, bark strips
Eggs: 4–8, white with small brown speckles
Incubation: 13–14 days, by female only
Nestling phase: 17–18 days
Fledgling phase: 4 or more weeks
Broods: 1–2
Migration: Generally a year-round resident

WARBLER

Prothonotary Warbler — *Protonotaria citrea*

Specialized Habitat

Prothonotary warblers are very specific in their nesting habitat requirements. About 75 percent of the time they nest in trees at the edge of, or even in, water. They prefer the borders of creeks and rivers, but also nest over still water in riverine floodplains.

The birds use natural cavities and woodpecker holes when no bird boxes are available. Of woodpecker cavities, those of downy woodpeckers are used most often, possibly because these have entrance holes about 1¼ to 1½ inches in diameter, a size the warblers seem to prefer. The average height of their nests in the wild is 4 to 6 feet above ground.

Cowbirds and Prothonotary Warblers

Cowbirds parasitize other birds by laying their eggs in other species' nests. The other species then incubates and raises the young cowbird as if it was one of its own. Cowbirds do not build nests or raise their own young.

In general, cowbirds are not *known* to parasi-

Quick Guide
Prothonotary Warbler

Breeding period: April through June
Territory size: Probably about 2–4 acres
Nest materials: Twigs, moss, lichens, fine
    grasses, leaves
Eggs: 4–6, white with many irregular
    brown spots
Incubation: 12–14 days, by female only
Nestling phase: 10–11 days
Fledgling phase: About 2 weeks
Broods: 1–2
Migration: Migrates to Central and South
    America

Prothonotary Warbler Birdhouse

Dimensions
Entrance-hole diameter:
    1¼"–1½"
Height of hole above floor: 5"–7"
Inside floor dimensions:
    4" x 4" to 5" x 5"
Total height of box: 9"–12"

Placement
Habitat: Right at the edge or slightly over
    the water of wooded creeks or rivers
Height: 4'–6' up on a tree or post

---

tize many cavity-nesting birds. This may be because they actually do not, owing to the small size of some of the cavity entrances; or it may be that this behavior has simply not yet been recorded because there have been fewer large-scale studies of cavity-nesting species. In any case, major studies of prothonotary warblers show that cowbirds parasitize as much as 23 percent of the nests.

Warblers and Birdhouses

There are only two species of North American warblers that nest in tree cavities. They are the prothonotary warbler and Lucy's warbler. The Lucy's warbler also lives along streams, but its range is restricted to the Southwest. It is not known to nest in birdhouses, but, then again, people may not have tried to attract it by putting up many appropriate birdhouses in its range and habitat.

The prothonotary warbler has been more actively courted by birdhouse enthusiasts. A pair will often use the same birdhouse for two broods in a single season. There is one record of three different pairs, each banded, using the same birdhouse to raise their broods, one pair after another, in a single season.

Prothonotary warbler, male.
Recognized by its all-yellow head and breast and blue-gray wings. Male is a bright golden yellow; female is greenish yellow.

WOODPECKERS

Downy Woodpecker — *Picoides pubescens*
Golden-fronted Woodpecker — *Melanerpes aurifrons*
Hairy Woodpecker — *Picoides villosus*
Northern Flicker — *Colaptes auratus*
Red-bellied Woodpecker — *Melanerpes carolinus*
Red-headed Woodpecker — *Melanerpes erythrocephalus*

Primary versus Secondary Cavity Nesters

As explained in the chapter "What Size House?" there are two types of cavity nesters — primary cavity nesters, which excavate their own cavities, and secondary cavity nesters, which use already existing holes. Secondary cavity nesters are obvious candidates for birdhouses, but do primary cavity nesters ever use birdhouses? The answer is sometimes they do and sometimes they don't.

All of our North American woodpeckers are primary cavity nesters and can quite easily make their own nest holes each year. In some cases, the actual excavating may be an important part of their breeding cycle, so much so that they will never accept a birdhouse. These birds often even excavate new nest holes on the same tree as last year's nest hole, rather than reuse the old one.

Northern Flicker Birdhouse

Dimensions
Entrance-hole diameter: 2"–3"
Height of hole above floor:
   10"–20"
Inside floor dimensions:
   6" x 6" to 8" x 8"
Total height of box: 14"–24"

Placement
Habitat: In or at the edge of open woods
Height: 10'–20' up on a tree or post

Red-headed woodpecker.
Recognized by its all-red head and neck and white belly. Male and female look alike.

Quick Guide
Red-headed Woodpecker

Breeding period: April into August
Territory size: 1–2 acres or more
Nest materials: None
Eggs: 4–5, pure white
Incubation: 12–13 days, by male and female
Nestling phase: About 30 days
Fledgling phase: 2–3 weeks
Broods: 1–2
Migration: Migrates from northern areas
   to southern United States

Northern flicker, female feeding nestling. Recognized by its brown back, black bib, and spotted breast. Males have a black or red "whisker" at the side of the mouth; females do not.

Which Woodpeckers Are Most Likely to Use Birdhouses?

For most of the species of North American woodpeckers there are very few or no reports of their using birdhouses. However, a few species fairly regularly do so. These include the northern flicker, red-bellied woodpecker, golden-fronted woodpecker, and red-headed woodpecker. To a much lesser extent, one may attract a hairy woodpecker and, rarely, a downy woodpecker.

The attractiveness of birdhouses to some other species of woodpeckers has not been tested, since they live in remote northern, mountain, or desert regions where fewer birdhouses have been put up. Perhaps with more experimentation we may find that other species of woodpeckers will accept birdhouses.

**Red-bellied wood-
pecker.**
Recognized by its black-
and-white striped back
and red cap. On male,
red cap extends to the
base of the bill; on fe-
male, it is just on back of
head.

Enlarging Entrances

In some cases, woodpeckers seem compelled to enlarge birdhouse entrances before they use them.
This is particularly true of red-bellied and red-
headed woodpeckers. Sometimes it may be done
in order for them to fit through the entrance com-
fortably; at other times, it may simply reflect the
bird's need to excavate. Occasionally, the exca-
vated chips become the nest-box lining, a prereq-
uisite for woodpecker birdhouses since the birds
do not bring in nesting material of their own.

Woodpecker Birdhouse
Golden-fronted Woodpecker
Hairy Woodpecker
Red-bellied Woodpecker
Red-headed Woodpecker

Dimensions
Entrance-hole diameter:
 1¾"–2¾"
Height of hole above floor: 10"–14"
Inside floor dimensions: 5" x 5" to 6" x 6"
Total height of box: 14"–16"

Placement
Habitat: In or at the edge of woods
Height: 6'–20' up on a tree, fence post, or
 building

Special Birdhouses for Woodpeckers

There are adjustments to a normal birdhouse that
may make it more attractive to woodpeckers. The
first is 1 to 2 inches of wood chips in the bottom
of the box. As mentioned above, woodpeckers do
not add any nesting material to their natural
homes, but they do leave an inch or two of wood
chips in the bottom of the cavity.

The chips may have several functions. They
may help to keep the eggs from rolling about the
bottom of the nest; they may help to keep the eggs
warm, since woodpeckers often partially bury
their eggs in the chips; and they may help to keep
some of the droppings of the young from contact
with their feathers and thus help in nest sanitation. It is probably better to use wood chips rather
than sawdust, since sawdust has a tendency to
absorb moisture and then mat and not dry out.

Other people feel that if the nest has natural
bark on the front it may be more attractive to
woodpeckers. There is no real proof of this.

A unique way to make a woodpecker house is
to take a log about 4 or 5 inches in diameter and
about 2 feet long; cut it in half lengthwise; hollow
out a cavity in the center about 12 inches long
and 4 inches in diameter; drill an entrance hole;
and then fasten the two sides of the log back together again. Basically you are trying to create a

Golden-fronted woodpecker, male.
Recognized by the golden-orange patch on the back of
its head. Male has a red patch on top of its head; the
female does not.

Quick Guide
Northern Flicker

Breeding period: April into July
Territory size: The area around the nest
Nest materials: None
Eggs: 7–9, pure white
Incubation: 11–12 days, by male and female
Nestling phase: About 26 days
Fledgling phase: 2–3 weeks
Broods: 1–2
Migration: Migrates from northern areas
　　to southern United States

Quick Guide
Golden-fronted Woodpecker
Red-bellied Woodpecker

Breeding period: April into July
Territory size: 3–4 acres
Nest materials: None
Eggs: 4–5, pure white
Incubation: 12–14 days, by male and female
Nestling phase: 25–30 days
Fledgling phase: 2 months or longer
Broods: 2, possibly 3
Migration: Red-bellied may migrate south
　　from northern parts of its range; golden-
　　fronted is year-round resident.

Downy woodpecker, male.
Recognized by white streak down back and short bill. Male has red patch on head; female does not.

Quick Guide
Downy Woodpecker

Breeding period: April into July
Territory size: Defends about ¼ acre around the nest, but ranges over a much larger area
Nest materials: None
Eggs: 4–5, pure white
Incubation: 12 days, by male and female
Nestling phase: 20–22 days
Fledgling phase: 2–3 weeks
Broods: 1, occasionally 2 in the South
Migration: Generally a year-round resident

Downy Woodpecker Birdhouse

Dimensions
Entrance-hole diameter:
    1¼″–1½″
Height of hole above floor:
    8″–12″
Inside floor dimensions:
    3″ x 3″ to 4″ x 4″
Total height of box: 10″–14″

Placement
Habitat: In or at the edge of woods
Height: 6′–20′ up on a tree

natural cavity through human labor. We have done this several times and have been very successful at attracting chickadees, but no woodpeckers.

Roost Holes for Winter

Many reports indicate that woodpeckers use nest boxes as roost holes during winter. Many cavity-nesting birds share this same behavior. Downy woodpeckers may be more likely to use a birdhouse as a roost than as a nesting site. This is a good reason to get your woodpecker houses up in fall.

How Much Wood Does a Woodpecker Peck?

Many people are concerned about having woodpeckers around their houses, fearing that they will peck large holes in their walls. Before you get too worried, you should know the basic facts about woodpecker pecking.

Basically, woodpeckers do three different types of pecking. Loud, rapid volleys on resonant surfaces, such as hollow trees or even house drainpipes, are called "drumming." This type of pecking does not involve any chipping away of wood; rather, it is a signal of territorial ownership, or mate advertisement, or a way for a mated pair to keep track of each other's whereabouts. Drumming will do no damage and occurs for only a short time in spring.

Hairy woodpecker. Similar to the smaller downy woodpecker, but with proportionately larger bill. Male has red patch on head; female does not.

Softer, irregular tapping is generally part of feeding behavior. Woodpeckers chip away tree bark in order to get at insects underneath. Usually, the larger the woodpecker, the bigger the chips. Most of our woodpeckers peck only small chips from the surface of wood while feeding. However, our largest woodpecker, the pileated woodpecker, can make holes several feet long and several inches wide and deep.

The final kind of pecking is nest-hole excavation. Most woodpeckers excavate in softer or partially rotted dead trees. The sound of this pecking is louder, slower, and more regular than that of feeding and continues for long periods of time, coming from the same place.

Snagging a Woodpecker

One of the best things that you can do to attract woodpeckers actually involves less rather than more work. Instead of getting all the deadwood trimmed out of your trees, leave it there, as long as it does not endanger anyone.

Dead branches on trees are called snags, and they serve two purposes for woodpeckers. First, they attract the kinds of insects that the woodpeckers eat. Second, they provide soft wood in which the woodpeckers can excavate their nest holes. Once the woodpeckers leave their nests, other species of cavity-nesting birds can use the empty holes. Thus, preserving snags and dead trees that are still standing is one of the most important conservation efforts you can make on your own property.

Some people try to increase the attractiveness of snags as nesting sites for woodpeckers by partially drilling 1-inch-diameter or larger holes into the deadwood. This may stir a woodpecker into thinking that this is a good place to start a nest cavity.

Quick Guide
Hairy Woodpecker

Breeding period: April through June
Territory size: Defends about ¼ acre around the nest, but ranges over a much larger area
Nest materials: None
Eggs: 4–6, pure white
Incubation: 11–12 days, by male and female
Nestling phase: 28–30 days
Fledgling phase: A few days
Broods: 1
Migration: Generally a year-round resident

WRENS

Bewick's Wren — *Thryomanes bewickii*
Carolina Wren — *Thryothorus ludovicianus*
House Wren — *Troglodytes aedon*

Welcome Songsters

All three of these wrens have wonderful songs that are a delightful addition to any backyard. The song of the house wren is like a bubbly waterfall, while that of the Bewick's wren is surprisingly similar to that of the song sparrow, a beautiful trail of notes that is impossible to describe.

The song of the Carolina wren is more easily described. Many catchy phrases have been used to imitate it, such as "teakettle, teakettle, teakettle," "sweetheart, sweetheart, sweetheart," or "sweet William, sweet William, sweet William."

All of these songs are given only by the males, and this can help you to determine which member of a pair you are watching, for the sexes look alike. Both male and female give the common, dry, rattle sound — a scolding call that seems to be shared by all wrens.

Most singing occurs in late winter and spring when the birds are actively courting and setting up territories. However, the Carolina wren can be heard singing to some extent in any month of the year.

Quick Guide
Carolina Wren

Breeding period: March through July
Territory size: About ½ to 1 acre
Nest materials: Weeds, leaves, grasses, bark strips, lined with feathers, moss, hair, fine grasses, and wool
Eggs: 5–6, white, heavily speckled with light brown
Incubation: 12–14 days, by female only
Nestling phase: 12–14 days
Fledgling phase: About 2 weeks
Broods: 2–3
Migration: Generally a year-round resident

Wren Birdhouse

Dimensions
Entrance-hole diameter:
    House wren, 1"–1½"
    Bewick's wren, 1¼"–1½"
    Carolina wren, 1½"
Height of hole above floor: 6"–7"
Inside floor dimensions:
    4" x 4" to 5" x 5"
Total height of box: 9"–12"

Placement
Habitat: Suburban yards, or open areas with a mixture of trees and dense shrubbery, or brush piles
Height: 4'–10' up on a tree, post, or building

No Place Like Home

The Carolina and Bewick's wrens are very flexible in their criteria for a nest site. Both may build nests in cavities or in dense shrubbery. In choosing cavities they may use a woodpecker home, a rotted-out knothole, or a variety of other crevices occurring around objects built by humans, such as the holes in fence posts.

Both of these wrens are also well known for choosing unusual nesting circumstances. For example, Carolina wrens have been found nesting in discarded tin cans and coffeepots, in baskets and pitchers, in cardboard boxes and mailboxes, and even in an abandoned hornets' nest.

The Bewick's wren has been found nesting in many of the same places, as well as in oil wells, deserted cars, or clothing hung on lines to dry. They have also used broken bottles, old hats, the skulls of cows in old fields, and the abandoned nests of mockingbirds and orioles.

Carolina wren.
Recognized by its brown back, buff belly, and clear,
white eyestripe. Male and female look alike.

He's No Dummy

House wrens are different in their nesting habits. They tend to prefer cavities and rarely build in the open. They also are more likely to look for a cavity in a tree or building and less likely to nest in odd bits of trash as the Carolina and Bewick's wrens do.

Another fascinating habit of the house wren is that the male starts building the nest before the female arrives. He stuffs the bird box full of twigs, sometimes to the point where he can barely get in. If he finds other nest cavities or birdhouses on his territory, he may start to build nests in these as well. These are sometimes referred to as "dummy" nests. Then when the female arrives, she chooses one of the nests and adds the final lining.

Why the male goes to all of this extra trouble is not known for sure, but there are several theories. One is that the abundance of nests may help to attract the female, leading her to believe that the male is particularly industrious or showing that this is an area abundant in nest cavities. Another theory suggests that the male may be trying to monopolize all available nest cavities.

In this way he keeps out other house wrens and other species that compete for nest holes and similar food. This same building of dummy nests has also been reported for the Bewick's wren.

Because of this habit, a single wren can use up 2 or 3 of your birdhouses, leaving fewer available for other cavity-nesting birds. You can solve this problem in two ways. One is to put up more boxes. The other is to watch the wren and get an idea of the boundaries of its territory, for it is only about a half-acre. Once you know his territory, move one or more of your boxes outside of that area.

Bewick's wren.
A dark wren, with a long tail, white belly, and thin, white eyestripe. Male and female look alike.

> *Quick Guide*
> **Bewick's Wren**
>
> *Breeding period:* March into August
> *Territory size:* Probably about ½ acre
> *Nest materials:* Twigs and grass, lined with grass and feathers
> *Eggs:* 5–7, white background, heavily speckled with light brown
> *Incubation:* 12–14 days, by female only
> *Nestling phase:* 14 days
> *Fledgling phase:* 2–3 weeks
> *Broods:* 1, possibly 2
> *Migration:* Generally a year-round resident, but some winter movement into southeast United States

Protective Nester

Wrens are quick to give scolding calls at the slightest sign of danger. The scolding call is a drawn-out rattling sound. If you are anywhere near the nest, the male or female will come out and scold. Sometimes this is a good way to locate a nest — if a wren is scolding you, chances are that you are close to a nest, or that fledglings are in nearby bushes.

Tail-Up

Many field guides show wrens with their tails up in the air or even suggest that this may be a field clue to their identification. However, most of the time wrens have their tails down, in the same position as most other birds'. It is only when they are disturbed that their tails point up.

In fact, tail-up is part of wren language for expressing disturbance or alarm. Another part of the wren's gestural language is a rapid quivering of its wings. This occurs when the male and female come close together during courtship and during interactions at the nest.

Winter

The house wren migrates south for the winter, but the Carolina wren and, in some parts of its range, the Bewick's wren stay on their territories throughout the winter. They both habitually

House wren.
A small, compact bird with a brown back and light, un-streaked belly. Body large in relation to tail. Male and female look alike.

roost in protected spots during these cold months, probably because they are not entirely winter-hardy. They have been known to roost in hornets' nests and in enclosed porches where there is an accessible opening. They will also roost in birdhouses, so this is a good reason to get your birdhouses up early and have them up in all seasons.

Both of these species tend to expand their range slightly during mild winters, which is probably a result of young birds' dispersing to new areas. Cold winters, however, take a toll on these birds. They are not usually found breeding in the same areas when spring arrives.

Quick Guide
House Wren

Breeding period: April into August
Territory size: ½ to ¾ acre
Nest materials: Base of straight twigs, lined with grasses and spider egg cases
Eggs: 5–6, white background, densely speckled with light brown
Incubation: 12–15 days, by female only
Nestling phase: 16–17 days
Fledgling phase: 14 days
Broods: 1–2
Migration: Migrates to southern North America

RESOURCES

Books about Birdhouses

Henderson, Carrol L. *Woodworking for Wildlife.* St. Paul, MN: Minnesota Department of Natural Resources Nongame Wildlife Program.

Kress, Stephen W. 1985. *The Audubon Society Guide to Attracting Birds.* New York: Charles Scribner's Sons.

Schultz, Walter E. 1970. *How to Attract, House and Feed Birds.* New York: Macmillan.

Scott, Virgil E., Keith E. Evans, David R. Patton, and Charles P. Stone. 1977. *Cavity-Nesting Birds of North American Forests.* Washington, DC: USDA Forest Service Agriculture Handbook 511.

Sorlie, Kip, and Richard Schinkel. 1988. *Building for Birds.* Drummond Island, MI: Generations.

Bird Magazines

Birder's World, 720 East 8th St., Holland, MI 49423.

Bird Watcher's Digest, Box 110, Marietta, OH 45750.

Living Bird Quarterly, Laboratory of Ornithology, Cornell University, 159 Sapsucker Woods Rd., Ithaca, NY 14850.

Wild Bird, P.O. Box 6040, Mission Viejo, CA 92690.

Bird Guides

Peterson, Roger Tory. 1980. *A Field Guide to the Birds.* Boston: Houghton Mifflin.

————. 1972. *A Field Guide to Western Birds.* Boston: Houghton Mifflin.

Scott, Shirley L., ed. 1983. *Field Guide to the Birds of North America.* Washington, DC: National Geographic Society.

Stokes, Donald W. 1979. *A Guide to Bird Behavior,* Vol. I. Boston: Little, Brown.

Stokes, Donald W., and Lillian Q. Stokes. 1983. *A Guide to Bird Behavior,* Vol. II. Boston: Little, Brown.

————. 1989. *A Guide to Bird Behavior,* Vol. III. Boston: Little, Brown.

Manufacturers of Birdhouses

Aspects, Inc., 245 Child St., P.O. Box 408, Warren, RI 02885.

Audubon Workshop, Inc., 1501 Paddock Dr., Northbrook, IL 60062.

The Bird House, P.O. Box 722, Estacada, OR 97023.

Briggs Associates, Inc., 851–A4 Highway 224, Denver, CO 80229.

C&S Products, Inc., Box 848, Fort Dodge, IA 50501.

Chesapeake Creative Arts, P.O. Box 444, Riderwood, MD 21139.

Country Ecology, P.O. Box 59, Center Sandwich, NH 03227.

Dan Ogle's Mountain Crafts, Rt. 2, Box 194–A, Huskey's Grove Rd., Sevierville, TN 37862.

Duncraft, 33 Fisherville Rd., Penacook, NH 03303–9020.

Heath Manufacturing Co., 140 Mill St., Coopersville, MI 49404.

Holland's Woodworks, P.O. Box 69, Powers, OR 97466.

Hyde Bird Feeder Company, P.O. Box 168, Waltham, MA 02254.

Kellogg Inc., 322 East Florida St., Milwaukee, WI 53201.

Kinsman Co., River Road, Point Pleasant, PA 18950.

Marsh Creek, P.O. Box 928, Geneva, NY 14456.

May Engineering, P.O. Box 351, Troy, MO 63379.

North States Industries, Inc., 1200 Mendelssohn Ave., Suite 210, Minneapolis, MN 55427.

Northwest Birdhouse Company, 4155 North Chase Rd., Rathdrum, ID 83858.

Opus, P.O. Box 525, Bellingham, MA 02019.

Pennington Enterprises, Inc., P.O. Box 290, Madison, GA 30650.

Rubbermaid, Inc., 1147 Akron Rd., Wooster, OH 44691.

Salt Creek Birdhouses, 452 North Walnut, Wood Dale, IL 60191.

Towanda Bird House, 6405 East Kellogg, Wichita, KS 67207.

White's Birdhouse Company, 5153 Neff Lake Rd., Brooksville, FL 34601.

Wildlife Studio, 7 Patten Rd., Bedford, NH 03102.

Woodlink Ltd., P.O. Box 508, Mount Ayr, IA 50854.

Retail Mail-Order Catalogs Specializing in Bird Products

Audubon Park Company, Drawer W., Akron, CO 80720.

Audubon Workshop, Inc., 1501 Paddock Dr., Northbrook, IL 60062.

Barn Owl Gift Shop, 2509 Lakeshore Dr., Fennville, MI 49408.

The Brown Company, P.O. Box 277, Yagoo Pond Rd., West Kingston, RI 02892.

Duncraft, 33 Fisherville Rd., Penacook, NH 03303–9020.

Hyde Bird Feeder Company, P.O. Box 168, Waltham, MA 02254.

Old Elm Feed and Supplies, P.O. Box 825, 13400 Watertown Plank Rd., Elm Grove, WI 53122.

Ol' Sam Peabody Company, P.O. Box 316, Berrien Springs, MI 49103.

Wild Bird Supplies, 4815 Oak St., Crystal Lake, IL 60012.

The Wood Thrush Shop, 992 Davidson Dr., Nashville, TN 37205.

Predator Controls

Audubon Workshop, Inc., 1501 Paddock Dr., Northbrook, IL 60062: raccoon and snake guards, and sparrow traps.

Bluebird Recovery Program, Audubon Chapter of Minneapolis, P.O. Box 566, Minneapolis, MN 55458: send $5.00 for information packet on bluebirds, including information on sparrow traps.

Harry Kruegar, Rt. 2, Box OR28, Ore City, TX 75683: will send you plans for snake guard if you send self-addressed, legal-size envelope with $.45 worth of stamps and $1.00 to cover cost of diagrams.

Bird Societies

Nature Society, Purple Martin Junction, Griggsville, IL 62340.

North American Bluebird Society, Box 6295, Silver Spring, MD 20906.

Purple Martin Conservation Association, c/o Edinboro University of Pennsylvania Institute for Research and Community Services, Edinboro, PA 16444.

NEST RECORD CARD

Nest box #_____

Species of bird: _____

Birds first enter box (date) _____

Start of nest building (date) _____

First egg (date) _____

Total number of eggs _____

First hatching (date) _____

Number of eggs hatched _____

First young fledged (date) _____

Number of young fledged _____

Comments: _____
_____
_____
_____
_____